CAPITAL PUNISHMENT — CRUEL AND UNUSUAL?

INFORMATION PLUS
WYLIE, TEXAS 75098
© 1979, 1982, 1984, 1990, 1992, 1994, 1996
ALL RIGHTS RESERVED

EDITORS:
NANCY R. JACOBS, B.A., M.A.
ALISON LANDES, B.A
MARK A. SIEGEL, M.A., Ph.D.

CHAPTER I

A CONTINUING CONFLICT — A HISTORY OF CAPITAL PUNISHMENT IN AMERICA

THE COLONIAL PERIOD

Since the first European settlers arrived in America, the death penalty has been accepted as just punishment for a variety of offenses. The English Penal Code, which applied to the British colonies, listed 14 capital offenses, but actual practice varied from colony to colony. In the Massachusetts Bay Colony, 13 crimes warranted the death penalty: idolatry, witchcraft, blasphemy, rape, statutory rape, kidnaping, perjury in a trial involving a possible death sentence, rebellion, murder, assault in sudden anger, adultery, and buggery (sodomy). In the statute, each crime was accompanied by an appropriate biblical quotation justifying the capital punishment. Later, arson, treason, and grand larceny were added.

In contrast, the Quakers adopted much milder laws. The Royal Charter for South Jersey (1646) did not permit capital punishment for any crime, and there was no execution until 1691. In Pennsylvania, William Penn's Great Act of 1682 limited the death penalty to treason and murder. Most states, however, followed the much harsher British codes.

THE FIRST ABOLITIONIST
OF THE DEATH PENALTY

Although the Founding Fathers commonly accepted the death penalty, many early Americans opposed capital punishment. In the late eighteenth century, Dr. Benjamin Rush (1745-1813), considered to be the founder of the American abolitionist movement, decried capital punishment. He attracted the support of Benjamin Franklin, and it was at Franklin's home in Philadelphia that Rush became one of the first Americans to propose a "House of Reform," a prison where criminals could be detained until they learned to change their antisocial behavior. Consequently, in 1790, the Walnut Street Jail was built in Philadelphia, the primitive seed from which the American penal system grew. (See *Prisons and Jails*, Information Plus, Wylie, TX, 1995.)

Dr. Rush published numerous pamphlets, the most noted of which was "Inquiry into the Justice and Policy of Punishing Murder by Death." Rush argued that the biblical support given capital punishment was questionable and that the threat of hanging did not deter crime and, in fact, might increase it. Reflecting the philosophy of the Enlightenment (the Age of Reason in the mid- to late 1700s), Rush believed the state exceeded its granted powers when it executed a citizen. In addition to Franklin, Rush attracted many other Pennsylvanians to his cause, including Pennsylvania's attorney general, William Bradford. As a result, Pennsylvania repealed the death penalty for all crimes except first-degree murder.

THE ABOLITIONIST MOVEMENT

Rush's proposals attracted many followers, and numerous abolitionist petitions were presented in states such as Ohio, New Jersey, New York, and Massachusetts, but no state reversed its laws. The second quarter of the nineteenth century was a time of reform in America, and capital punishment opponents rode the tide of righteousness and indignation created by the anti-saloon and antislavery advocates. Abolitionist societies sprang up, most notably along the Atlantic coast, and in 1845, the American Society for the Abolition of Capital Punishment was founded.

In the late 1840s, Horace Greeley, the editor and founder of the *New York Tribune* and a leading advocate of most abolitionist causes, became a leader in the crusade against the death penalty. Finally, in 1846, the Territory of Michigan abolished the death penalty and replaced it with life imprisonment. The law took effect the following year, making Michigan, for all practical purposes, the first English-speaking jurisdiction in the world to abolish the death penalty for common crimes. (It retained it for treason.) In 1852, Rhode Island included even treason when it outlawed hanging, as did Wisconsin a year later. Most states began limiting the number of capital crimes. In fact, outside the South, murder and treason became the only acts warranting capital punishment.

Opponents of the death penalty initially benefited from abolitionist sentiment, but as the Civil War neared, concern about the death penalty was lost amid the growing antislavery movement. It was not until after the Civil War that Maine and Iowa abolished the death penalty, but almost immediately their legislatures reversed themselves and reinstated it. In 1887, Maine again reversed itself and abolished capital punishment. Colorado also abolished capital punishment, but apparently against the will of many of its citizens. At least twice they lynched convicted murderers, and in response, Colorado restored the penalty.

Meanwhile, the federal government, following considerable debate, reduced the number of federal crimes punishable by death to three — treason, murder, and rape. In no instance was it to be mandatory.

A DECLINE IN ABOLITIONIST FORTUNES

At the turn of the century, death-penalty abolitionists again rode the tide of American reformism as the Progressives (liberal reformers) tried to correct the deficiencies of the American system. Between 1907 and 1917, nine states and Puerto Rico outlawed capital punishment, but the momentum failed to last. By 1921, five states had reinstated it. The Prohibition Era, characterized by frequent disdain for law and order, almost destroyed the abolitionist movement.

Only the determined efforts of the famed Clarence Darrow, the "attorney for the damned"; Lewis E. Lawes, the abolitionist warden of Sing-Sing Prison (New York); and the American League to Abolish Capital Punishment, founded in 1927, prevented the movement's complete collapse. Nonetheless, of the 16 states and jurisdictions (including Puerto Rico) that outlawed capital punishment after 1845, only seven — Michigan, Rhode Island, Wisconsin, Maine, North Dakota, Minnesota, and Puerto Rico — had no major death-penalty statute entering the 1950s. In fact, between 1917 and 1957 no state abolished the death penalty.

The movement made a mild comeback in the mid-1950s, and the issue was discussed in several state legislatures. However, only the (then) territories of Alaska and Hawaii (1957) abolished the death penalty. The movement's singular success in Delaware (1958) was reversed only three years later (1961), a major disappointment for the opponents of the death penalty. Nonetheless, the abolitionists were able to recover during the Civil Rights movement of the 1960s. Michigan (1963, for treason), Oregon (1964), Iowa (1965), and West Virginia (1965) all abolished capital punishment, while many other states sharply reduced the number of crimes warranting the death penalty. Only Oregon has since reinstated capital punishment. As of 1995, 38 states, the federal government, and the U.S. military have the death penalty. (See Chapter V.)

The federal government no longer lists rape as one of the crimes punishable by death, but it continues to impose the death penalty for murder, treason, and espionage. Over the years, the federal government has added to the number of crimes punishable by the death penalty. Between 1977 and 1994, Congress enacted four more death penalty statutes. In 1994, the Violent Crime Control and Law Enforcement Act of 1994 (PL 103-322) made more than 50 offenses punishable by death.

RESOLVING THE CONSTITUTIONAL ISSUES

Until the 1960s, there was legally no question that the death penalty was acceptable under the United States Constitution. Then, in 1963, Justice Arthur Goldberg (joined by Justices Douglas and Brennan), dissenting to a rape case in which the defendant had been sentenced to death (*Rudolph v. Alabama* [375 US 889, 1963]), raised the question of the legality of the death penalty. The filing of a large number of cases in the late 1960s led to an implied moratorium on carrying out the death penalty, which lasted until 1977, when the state of Utah executed a convicted murderer.

Since 1972 with *Furman v. Georgia* (408 US 238) and the accompanying cases, the Supreme Court has been defining and refining what is and is not acceptable under the U.S. Constitution. With the replacement of Chief Justice Earl Warren by Chief Justice Warren Burger and his later replacement by Chief Justice William Rehnquist, the court majority has generally interpreted the death penalty as worthy of extra attention because of the seriousness of the consequences, but most assuredly as acceptable punishment for murder. (See Chapter II.) There can be little question that the High Court position reflects that of the American public. (See Chapter VII.) (See Chapters II, III, and IV for court rulings on capital punishment.)

WORLDWIDE TREND

The *de facto* moratorium between 1967 and 1977 paralleled a general worldwide movement, especially among Western nations, towards the abolition of capital punishment. While the United States resumed executions during the late 1970s, most of the Western world was either formally or informally abolishing it. Today, among the Western democratic nations with which the United States traditionally compares itself, only the United States imposes the death penalty. (There are technical exceptions — Israel, for example, despite continuing conflict, maintains the death penalty for "crimes against mankind" but has executed only Adolf Eichmann. Some countries still maintain the death penalty for treason — although no Western democracy has actually imposed it.) One of the first acts of the parliaments of many of the Eastern European countries after the fall of Communism was to abolish capital punishment. In 1992, the government of South Africa stopped executing prisoners, and in 1995, its Supreme Court abolished the death penalty. (See Chapter IX.)

CHAPTER II

CRUEL AND UNSUAL?
SUPREME COURT RULINGS

In 1967, a coalition of anti-death penalty groups brought suit on a variety of constitutional grounds against Florida and California, the states with the most inmates on death row. The suit led to a *de facto* moratorium until the issues could be decided. This moratorium lasted until 1977 when Gary Gilmore, virtually at his own request, was executed by the State of Utah.

"AS THE STATUTES ARE ADMINISTERED"

On June 29, 1972, a split 5-4 Supreme Court reached the landmark decision, *Furman v. Georgia* (408 US 238 — which included *Jackson v. Georgia* and *Branch v. Texas*), which held that "as the statutes are administered ... the imposition and carrying out of the death penalty [constitutes] cruel and unusual punishment in violation of the Eighth and Fourteenth Amendments." Within both the majority opinions and the minority opinions, the justices could not agree on the arguments explaining why they supported or opposed the death penalty. Justice Douglas, in his concurring majority opinion, quoted former Attorney General Ramsey Clark,

> It is the poor, the sick, the ignorant, the powerless, and the hated who are executed.... [The law] leaves to the uncontrolled discretion of judges and juries the determination whether defendants committing these crimes should die or be imprisoned.... these discretionary statutes are unconstitutional.

Justice Brennan stated that

> at bottom, the Cruel and Unusual Punishments Clause prohibits the infliction of uncivilized and inhumane punishments. The State, even as it punishes, must treat its members with respect, for their intrinsic worth as human beings. A punishment is "cruel and unusual" therefore if it does not comport with human dignity.... the deliberate extinguishment of human life by the State is uniquely degrading to human dignity.

Justice Stewart stressed another point.

> These death sentences are cruel and unusual in the same way that being struck by lightning is cruel and unusual. For of all the people convicted of rapes and murders are among a capriciously selected random handful upon whom the sentence of death has in fact been imposed.... I simply conclude that the Eighth and Fourteenth Amendments cannot tolerate the infliction of sentence of death under legal systems that permit this unique penalty to be so wantonly and so freakishly imposed.

That did not mean that Justice Stewart would rule out the death penalty if a more equitable system were found in applying this severe penalty. Indeed, he saw the death penalty as justified.

> The instinct for retribution is part of the nature of man, and channeling that instinct in the administration of criminal justice serves an important purpose in promoting the stability of a society governed by law. When people begin to believe that organized society is unwilling or unable to impose upon criminal offenders the punishment they "deserve" then there are sown the seeds of anarchy — of self help, vigilante justice, and lynch law.

Justice White stated that "as it is presently administered, the penalty is so infrequently imposed that the threat of execution is too attenuated to be of substantial service to criminal justice." Justice Marshall concluded that "the death penalty is an excessive and unnecessary punishment which violates the Eighth Amendment.... it is morally unacceptable to the people of the United States at this time in their history."

Not Everyone Agreed

For the dissenters, Chief Justice Warren Burger observed that "the constitutional prohibition against 'cruel and unusual punishments' cannot be construed to bar the imposition of the punishment of death." Justice Blackmun feared "that statutes stricken down today will be reenacted by state legislatures to prescribe the death penalty for specified crimes without any alternative for the imposition of a lesser punishment in the discretion of the judge or jury." Justice Powell declared,

> I find no support in the language of the Constitution, in its history, or in the cases arising under it — for the view that this Court may invalidate a category of penalties because we deem less severe penalties adequate

> to serve the ends of penology ... if we were free to question the justification for the use of capital punishment, a heavy burden would be on those who attack the legislatures' judgments to prove the lack of rational justifications. This Court has long held that legislative decisions in this area, which are within the special competency of that branch, are entitled to the presumption of validity. (The Court would not question the validity of a government entity properly doing its job unless its actions were way out of line.)

Justice Rehnquist concurred.

> How can government by the elected representatives of the people coexist with the power of the federal judiciary whose members are constitutionally insulated from responsiveness to the popular will, to declare invalid laws duly enacted by the popular branches of government.

Only Justices Brennan and Marshall concluded that the Eighth Amendment prohibited the death penalty for every crime and under all circumstances. Justice Douglas's opinions did not necessarily require the final abolition of the penalty. Justices Stewart and White concluded that because of the capricious imposition of the sentence, the death penalty violated the Eighth Amendment. As a result, most state legislatures started rewriting their capital punishment laws to make them more equitable in order to swing the votes of Stewart and White (and later that of John Stevens, who replaced the retired Justice Douglas).

PROPER IMPOSITION
OF THE DEATH PENALTY

Four years later, on July 2, 1976, the High Court ruled decisively in a 7 to 2 decision on a

series of cases concerning the death penalty that the death penalty is, indeed, constitutional. With Brennan and Marshall dissenting, the Court stressed (just in case *Furman* had been misunderstood) that "the death penalty is not a form of punishment that may never be imposed, regardless of the circumstances of the offense, regardless of the procedure followed in reaching the decision." Furthermore, "the infliction of death as a punishment for murder is not without justification and ... is not unconstitutionally severe."

The ruling upheld death penalty statutes in Georgia, Florida, and Texas (*Gregg v. Georgia,* 428 US 153, the source of the quotes above; *Proffitt v. Florida,* 428 US 242; and *Jurek v. Texas,* 428 US 262); but struck down laws in North Carolina (*Woodson v. North Carolina,* 428 US 280) and Louisiana (*Roberts v. Louisiana,* 428 US 40) as being too rigid in requiring capital punishment for certain crimes. Referring to the acceptability of the new Georgia laws covering capital punishment in *Gregg v. Georgia,* Justice Stewart supported the bifurcated (two-part) trial system in which the jury first judges guilt, and then, upon the finding of guilt, separately considers whether the crime deserves the death penalty or whether mitigating circumstances exist to warrant a lesser sentence. This system meets the requirements demanded by *Furman*. Noting how the Georgia statutes fulfilled these demands, Justice Stewart observed,

> These procedures [established by the Georgia statutes] require the jury to consider the circumstances of the crime and the criminal before it recommends sentence. No longer can a Georgia jury do as Furman's jury did: reach a finding of the defendant's guilt and then, without guidance or direction, decide whether he should live or die. Instead, the jury's attention is directed to the specific "circumstances of the crime: Was it committed in the course of another capital felony? Was it committed for money? Was it committed upon a peace officer or judicial officer? Was it committed in a particularly heinous way or in a manner that endangered the lives of many persons?" In addition, the jury's attention is focused on the characteristics of the person who committed the crime: Does he have a record of prior convictions for capital offenses? Are there any special facts about this defendant that mitigate against imposing capital punishment (e.g., his youth, the extent of his cooperation with the police, his emotional state at the time of the crime)? As a result, while some jury discretion still exists, "the discretion to be exercised is controlled by clear and objective standards so as to produce non-discriminatory application."

In addition, the Georgia law required that all death sentences be automatically appealed to the state Supreme Court, an "important additional safeguard against arbitrariness and caprice."

In *Profitt v. Florida*, the High Court upheld Florida's death penalty laws, a system similar to Georgia's, except that in Florida the sentence was determined by the trial judge rather than by the jury, which had an advisory role with respect to the sentencing phase of the trial. The court found Florida sentencing guidelines adequate to prevent the unfair imposition of the death sentence.

CAN FUTURE CRIMINAL ACTIVITY BE PREDICTED?

In *Jurek v. Texas*, the issue centered on whether a jury can satisfactorily determine the future actions of a convicted murderer. (See Chapter IV for role of psychiatrists in determining future actions.) The Texas statutes required that during the sentencing phase of the trial, after the defendant has been found guilty, the jury determines "whether there is a probability that the defendant would commit criminal acts of violence that would constitute a continuing threat to society." Jurek's attorneys argued that "it is impossible to predict future behavior and that the question is so vague as to be meaningless." Justice Stewart agreed that "it is, of course, not easy to predict future behavior." Nonetheless,

> The fact that such a determination is difficult, however, does not mean that it cannot be made. Indeed, prediction of future criminal conduct is an essential element in many of the decisions rendered throughout our criminal justice system. The decision whether to admit a defendant to bail, for instance, must often turn on a judge's prediction of the defendant's future conduct. Any sentencing authority must predict a convicted person's probable future conduct when it engages in the process of determining what punishment to impose. For those sentenced to prison, these same predictions must be made by parole authorities. The task that a Texas jury must perform in answering the statutory question is thus basically no different from the task performed countless times each day throughout the American System of criminal justice.

FLEXIBLE GUIDELINES
FOR JUDGES AND JURORS

In *Woodson v. North Carolina* (and *Roberts v. Louisiana*), the court ruled that statutes requiring the death penalty for all those convicted of first-degree murder did not meet

> objective standards to guide, regularize, and make rationally reviewable the process for imposing the sentence of death.... [The statute] provides no standards to guide the jury in its inevitable exercise of the power to determine which first-degree murderer shall live and which shall die.

Furthermore, the North Carolina laws did not "allow the particularized consideration of relevant aspects of the character and record of each convicted defendant before the imposition upon him of a sentence of death." The court observed that the North Carolina statute "treats all persons convicted of a designated offense not as uniquely individual human beings, but as members of a faceless, undifferentiated mass to be subjected to the blind infliction of the penalty of death." Capital punishment, concluded the High Court, "requires consideration of the character and record of the individual offender and the circumstances of the particular offense as a constitutionally indispensable part of the process of inflicting the penalty of death."

The Louisiana mandatory death penalty for first-degree murder suffered from similar inadequacies. It did, however, permit the jury to consider lesser offenses such as second-degree murder. The Supreme Court rejected the Louisiana law because it forced the jury to find the defendant guilty of a lesser crime if it wanted to avoid giving the death penalty rather than having the option of finding the defendant guilty of first-degree murder, the crime he had actually committed, and then, based on mitigating circumstances, recommending life imprisonment rather than the death penalty.

As a result of either *Furman* or *Gregg*, or both, virtually every state's capital punishment statute had to be rewritten to provide flexible guidelines for judges and juries so that they might fairly decide capital cases and consider and impose, if necessary, the death penalty.

EXCLUSION FROM JURIES OF THOSE
AGAINST CAPITAL PUNISHMENT

In *Witherspoon v. Illinois* (391 US 510, 1967), the United States Supreme Court found unconstitutional the simple exclusion from juries of all who opposed the death penalty without trying to determine whether "their scruples would invariably compel them to vote against capital punishment." A selective process that eliminated all prospective jurors who opposed capital punishment would create a jury which "can speak only for a distinct and dwindling minority." It would not represent the community and would not be fair and impartial. "No defendant," concluded the Court, "can constitutionally be put to death at the hands of a tribunal so selected.... The State has stacked the deck against the [defendant]. To execute this death sentence would deprive him of his life without due process of law."

However, the findings in *Witherspoon* did not mean that no one opposing the death penalty could be excluded. A prospective juror had to

> be willing to *consider* all the penalties provided by state law, and that he not be irrevocably committed before the trial has begun, to vote against the penalty of death regardless of the facts and circumstances that might emerge in the course of proceedings.

The Supreme Court indicated that the trial court could exclude for cause prospective jurors

> who made unmistakably clear (1) that they would *automatically* vote against the imposition of capital punishment without regard to any evidence that might be developed at the trial ... or (2) that their attitudes toward the death penalty would prevent them from making an impartial decision as to the defendant's *guilt*.

Finally, the Court noted that based on "presently available knowledge,"

> We simply cannot conclude ... that the exclusion of jurors opposed to

capital punishment results in an unrepresentative jury on the issue of guilt or substantially increases the risk of conviction.

Consequently, based on *Witherspoon,* it has become the practice in most states, including Illinois, to exclude prospective jurors who indicate that they could not possibly, in good conscience, return a death penalty from juries which will try capital cases. In the *Lockett v. Ohio* (438 US 586, 1978, see Chapter III) the Supreme Court upheld *Witherspoon* when it dismissed *Lockett's* contention that the exclusion of four prospective jurors who opposed the death penalty denied her an impartial jury.

Weakening *Witherspoon*

In *Wainwright v. Witt* (469 US 412, 1985), a 7-2 Supreme Court majority eased the strict requirements of *Witherspoon.* Writing for the majority, Justice Rehnquist declared that the new capital punishment procedures left less discretion to jurors and that therefore, "the requirement that a juror may be excluded only if he would never vote for the death penalty is now missing; gone too is the extremely high burden of proof. In general, the standard has been simplified." Justice Rehnquist indicated that potential jurors in capital cases should be excluded from jury duty in a manner "no different" from how they were excluded in noncapital cases.

No longer would a juror's "automatic" bias against imposing the death penalty have to be proved with "unmistakable clarity." A prosecutor could not be expected to ask all the questions necessary to determine if a juror would "automatically" rule against the death penalty or fail to convict a defendant if he or she were likely to face execution. Fundamentally, the question of exclusion from a jury should be determined by the interplay of the prosecutor and the defense lawyer and the decision of the judge based on his initial observations of the prospective juror. These are the individuals who can see first-hand whether prospective jurors' beliefs would bias their ability to impose the death penalty.

In his dissent, Justice Brennan claimed that making it easier to eliminate those who opposed capital punishment from the jury created a jury not only more likely to impose the death sentence, but also more likely to convict. He also attacked the majority interpretation that now treated exclusion from a capital case as similar to exclusion from any other case.

IT DOES NOT MATTER IF "DEATH QUALIFIED" JURIES ARE MORE LIKELY TO CONVICT

In *Lockhart v. McCree* (476 US 162, 1986), the Supreme Court resolved the issue of a fair trial with a "death qualified" jury. Ardia McCree was convicted of murdering Evelyn Boughton while robbing her gift shop and service station in Camden, Arkansas. In accordance with Arkansas law, the trial judge removed eight prospective jurors from serving on the jury because they indicated they could not, under any circumstances, vote for imposition of the death sentence. The jury then convicted McCree, and, although the state sought the death penalty, sentenced McCree to life imprisonment without parole.

McCree appealed, claiming that the removal of the so-called "Witherspoon-excludables" violated his right to a fair trial under the Sixth and Fourteenth Amendments to have his guilt or innocence determined by an impartial jury selected from a representative cross-section of the community, which would include people strongly opposed to the death penalty. Both the Federal District Court and the Federal Court of Appeals agreed with McCree, but in a 6-3, decision, the Supreme Court did not.

The High Court majority did not accept the validity of the studies presented to show that those strongly opposed to the death penalty were less likely to convict and those who supported the death penalty were more likely to convict. Furthermore, stated Justice Rehnquist for the majority, even if they did accept the validity of these studies, "the Constitution does not prohibit the States from 'death qualifying' juries in capital cases." Certainly, observed Justice Rehnquist, excluding large groups, such as Blacks, women, or Mexican-Americans from the jury "undeniably gave rise to an 'appearance of unfairness.'" However, excluding "those who cannot and will not conscientiously obey the law [by sentencing a convicted murderer to death] ... hardly can be said to create an 'appearance of unfairness.'"

The majority also thought that the logical outcome of McCree's argument would be "both illogical and hopelessly impractical." If a balance between those supporting and those opposed to the death penalty were required, then the judge might have to make sure that each jury "contain[ed] the proper number of Democrats and Republicans, young persons and old persons, white-collar executive and blue-collar laborers and so on." Arkansas had done its best to select an impartial jury from a fair cross-section of the population and the exclusion of a small portion did not make this an unfair selection of jurors.

Writing in dissent, Justice Marshall observed that if the High Court thought in *Witherspoon* excluding those who opposed the death penalty meant that a convicted murderer did not get a fair hearing during the sentencing part of the trial, it would also logically mean that he or she would not get a fair hearing during the initial trial part. The Court minority generally accepted the studies showing "that 'death-qualification' in fact produces juries somewhat more 'conviction-prone' than 'non-death-qualified' juries."

CHOOSING A LESSER CHARGE

Along with an accomplice, Gilbert Beck entered the home of Roy Malone. While they were tying up the victim, Beck's accomplice unexpectedly struck and killed Malone. Beck admitted to the robbery, but claimed the murder was not part of the plan. Beck was tried under an Alabama statute for "robbery or attempts thereof when the victim is intentionally killed by the defendant."

Under Alabama law the judge was specifically prohibited from giving the jury the option of convicting the defendant of a lesser included offense. Instead, the jury was given the choice of either convicting the defendant of the capital crime, in which case it was required to impose the death penalty, or acquitting him, thus allowing him to escape all penalties for his alleged participation in the crime. The judge could not have offered the jury the lesser alternative of felony-murder, which did not deal with the accused's intentions at the time of the crime.

Beck appealed, claiming this law created a situation in which the jury was more likely to convict. The Supreme Court, in *Beck v. Alabama* (447 US 625, 1980), agreed and reversed the lower court's ruling. They observed that, while not a matter of due process, it was virtually universally accepted in lesser offenses that a third alternative be offered. "That safeguard" noted the Court,

> would seem to be especially important in a case such as this. For when the evidence unquestionably establishes that the defendant is guilty of a serious, violent offense — but leaves some doubt with respect to an element that would justify conviction of a capital offense — the failure to give the jury the "third option" of convicting on a lesser included offense would seem inevitably to enhance the risk of an unwarranted conviction.

According to the ruling, such a risk could not be tolerated in a case in which the defendant's life was at stake. *Beck*, however, did not require a jury to consider a lesser charge in every case, but only where the consideration would be justified *(Hooper v. Evans*, 456 US 605, 1982).

THE BUCK STOPS WITH THE JURY

During the course of a robbery, Bobby Caldwell shot and killed the owner of a grocery store. He was tried and found guilty. During the sentencing phase of the trial, Caldwell's attorney pleaded for mercy, concluding his summation by emphasizing to the jury

> ... I implore you to think deeply about this matter.... You are the judges and you will have to decide his fate. It is an awesome responsibility, I know — an awesome responsibility.

Responding to the defense attorney's plea, the prosecutor played down the responsibility of the jury, stressing the fact that a life sentence would be reviewed by a higher court.

> [The defense] would have you believe that your decision is the final decision. God, how unfair can they be? Your job is reviewable. [The defense] said this panel was going to kill this man. I think that's terribly unfair. [The defense is] insinuating that your decision is the final decision ... and that is terribly, terribly unfair. For they know, as I know, and as Judge Baker has told you, that the decision you render is automatically reviewable by the Supreme Court. Automatically.

The jury sentenced Caldwell to death and the case was automatically appealed. The Mississippi Supreme Court upheld the conviction, but split 4-4 on the validity of the death sentence, thereby upholding the death sentence by an equally divided court.

In a 5-3 decision (Justice Powell took no part in the decision), the U.S. Supreme Court, in *Caldwell v. Mississippi* (472 US 320, 1985), vacated (threw out) the death sentence. Writing for the majority, Justice Marshall noted that

> it is constitutionally impermissible to rest a death sentence on a determination made by a sentencer who has been led to believe that the responsibility for determining the appropri-

ateness of the defendant's death rests elsewhere.... [This court] has taken as a given that capital sentencers would view their task as the serious one of determining whether a specific human being should die at the hands of the State. [This is supposed to be a] truly awesome responsibility.

Furthermore, the appeals court was not the place to make this life and death decision.

Whatever intangibles a jury might consider in its sentencing determination, few can be gleaned from an appellate record. This inability to confront and examine the individuality of the defendant would be particularly devastating to any argument for consideration of what this Court has termed "[those] compassionate or mitigating factors stemming from the diverse frailties of humankind."

Most appellate courts presume that the sentencing was correctly done, which would leave the defendant at a distinct disadvantage. Furthermore, expecting to be reversed by an appeals court, a jury might choose to "send a message" of extreme disapproval for the defendant's acts and sentence him or her to death to show they will not tolerate such actions. Should the appeals court fail to reverse the decision, the defendant might be executed when the jury only intended to "send a message."

The three dissenting judges believed "the Court has overstated the seriousness of the prosecutor's comments" and that it was "highly unlikely that the jury's sense of responsibility was diminished."

JURY CONSIDERATIONS

In 1990, Jonathan Dale Simmons beat an elderly woman to death in her home in Columbia, South Carolina. The week before his capital murder trial began, he pleaded guilty to first degree burglary and two counts of criminal sexual conduct in connection with two prior assaults on elderly women. These guilty pleas resulted in convictions for violent offenses, and those convictions made him ineligible for parole if convicted of any other violent-crime offense. At the capital murder trial, over the defense counsel's objection, the trial court did not allow the defense to ask prospective jurors if they understood the meaning of a "life" sentence under South Carolina law. The prosecution also asked the judge not to mention parole through the trial. After three days of trial, the jury convicted Simmons of murder.

In the closing arguments, the prosecution argued that Simmons's dangerousness was a factor in sentencing. The defense argued that, due to Simmons' "unique psychological problems, his dangerousness was limited to elderly women" and "there was no reason to expect further acts of violence once he was isolated in a prison setting." Despite the jury asking for a definition, the judge did not allow instructions that if the defendant was sentenced to life imprisonment, he would not be eligible for parole. The judge told the jury that

> You are instructed not to consider parole or parole eligibility in reaching your verdict.... The terms life imprisonment and death sentence are to be understood in the plan [sic] and ordinary meaning,...

After 25 minutes of deliberation, the jury returned with a sentence of death. On appeal, the Supreme Court of South Carolina upheld the sentence.

The United States Supreme Court, in a 6-2 decision (*Simmons v. South Carolina* 62 LW 4509, 1994), overruled the South Carolina Court, concluding,

> Where a defendant's future dangerousness is at issue, and state law prohibits his release on parole, due

process requires that the sentencing jury be informed that the defendant is parole ineligible. An individual cannot be executed on the basis of information which he had no opportunity to deny or explain.... Petitioner's jury reasonably may have believed that he could be released on parole if he were not executed. To the extent that this misunderstanding pervaded its deliberations, it had the effect of creating a false choice between sentencing him to death and sentencing him to a limited period of incarceration. The trial court's refusal to apprise the jury of information so crucial to its determination, particularly when the State alluded to the defendant's future dangerousness in its argument, cannot be reconciled with this Court's well-established precedents interpreting the Due Process Clause.

JUDGE SENTENCING INSTEAD OF JURY

Florida uses a trifurcated (three-part) trial system to deal with capital cases. The jury decides the guilt or innocence of the accused. If the jury finds the defendant guilty, they then recommend an advisory opinion of either life imprisonment or the death sentence. The trial judge then considers aggravating and mitigating circumstances, weighs the two as if on a balance, and then, based on his or her findings, sentences the convicted murderer to either life or death.*

A Florida jury convicted Joseph Spaziano of torturing and murdering two women. The jury recommended Spaziano be sentenced to life imprisonment, but the trial judge, after considering the mitigating and aggravating circumstances, sentenced the defendant to death. Among several contentions included in the appeal, Spaziano claimed the judge's overriding of the jury's recommendation of life violated the Eighth Amendment's prohibition against "cruel and unusual punishment." The Supreme Court, in a 5-3 decision, in *Spaziano v. Florida* (468 US 447, 1984), did not agree.

Spaziano's lawyers claimed juries, not judges, were better equipped to make reliable capital-sentencing decisions and that a jury's decision for life imprisonment should be inviolate (not questioned). The reason for this was that the death penalty was unlike any other sentence and required that the jury have the ultimate word. This belief had been upheld, Spaziano claimed, because 30 out of 37 states with capital punishment had the jury decide the prisoner's fate. Furthermore, since the primary justification for the death penalty was retribution and an expression of community outrage, the jury served as the voice of the community and was in the best position to decide whether a particular crime was so terrible that the community's response must be death.

The High Court indicated that Spaziano's "argument obviously has some appeal," but contained two fundamental flaws. First, retribution played a role in all sentences, not just death sentences. Second, a jury was not the only source of community input. "The community's voice is heard at least as clearly in the legislature when the death penalty is authorized and the particular circumstances in which death is appropriate are defined." Trial judges sentencing defendants was a normal part of the judicial system. The Supreme Court continued,

---

*Of the 37 states with capital punishment in 1984, when *Spaziano v. Florida* was heard, 30 states had the jury decide the fate of the convicted murderer. In Arizona, Idaho, Montana, and Nebraska, the court alone imposed the sentence. Besides Florida, only Alabama and Indiana allowed a judge to override a jury's recommendation of life. Since 1972, when this method was introduced in Florida, judges have overridden a jury's recommendations of life imprisonment 82 times.

In light of the facts that the Sixth Amendment does not require jury sentencing, that the demands of fairness and reliability in capital cases do not require it, and that neither the nature of, nor the purpose behind, the death penalty requires jury sentencing, we cannot conclude that placing responsibility on the trial judge to impose the sentence in a capital case is unconstitutional.

In addition, just because 30 of 37 states chose to permit a jury to make the decision did not mean that those states that chose to let a judge make the decision were wrong. "As the Court several times has made clear, we are unwilling to say that there is any one right way for a State to set up its capital-sentencing scheme." Therefore, there was nothing wrong in a judge deciding on the applicability of the death penalty, even after the jury had advised the court to grant life imprisonment.

Writing for the dissenters, Justice Stevens indicated that

> because of its severity and irrevoca-bility, the death penalty is qualita-tively different from any other punishment, and hence must be accompanied by unique safeguards to ensure that it is a justified response to a given offense. Because it is the one punishment that cannot be prescribed by a rule of law as judges normally understand such rules, but rather is ultimately understood only as an expression of the community's outrage — its sense that an individual has lost his moral entitlement to live — I am convinced that the danger of an excessive response can only be avoided if the decision to impose the death penalty is made by a jury rather than by a single governmental official ... [because a jury] is best able to "express the conscience of the community on the ultimate question of life or death."

Justice Stevens also gave weight to the fact that 30 out of 37 states had the jury make the decision, referring to the "high level of consensus ... thereby demonstrating a strong community feeling that it is only decent and fair to leave the life-or-death decision to the authentic voice of the community — the jury — rather than to a single government official."

Advisory Juries

Louise Harris had asked a co-worker, Lorenzo McCarter, with whom she was having an affair, to find someone to kill her husband. McCarter paid two accomplices $100.00, with a vague promise of more after they killed the husband. McCarter testified against Harris in exchange for the prosecutor's promise that he would not seek the death penalty against him. He testified that Harris had asked him to kill her husband so they could share in his death benefits. An Alabama jury convicted Louise Harris of capital murder. At the sentencing hearing, witnesses testified to her good background and strong character. She was rearing seven children, held three jobs simultaneously, and participated in her church.

Alabama law gives capital sentencing author-ity to the trial judge, but requires the judge to "consider" an advisory jury verdict. The jury voted 7 to 5 that she be imprisoned for life without parole. The trial judge then considered her sentence, finding the existence of one aggravating circumstance (the murder was committed for monetary gain), one statutory mitigating circum-stance (Harris had no prior criminal record), and one nonstatutory mitigating circumstance (Harris was a hard-working, respected member of her church).

Noting that she had planned the crime, financed it, and stood to benefit from the murder, the judge felt that the aggravating circumstance outweighed the other mitigating circumstances and sentenced her to death. On appeal, the Alabama Supreme Court affirmed the conviction and sentence and rejected Harris's arguments that the procedure was unconstitutional because Alabama state law did "not specify the weight the judge must give to the jury's recommendation and thus permits the arbitrary imposition of the death penalty."

The case was then appealed to the Supreme Court of the United States, which upheld the Alabama court's decision. In *Harris v. Alabama* (63 LW 4148, 1995), the high court ruled that the Eighth Amendment did not require a state "to define the weight the sentencing judge must give to an advisory jury verdict."

> Because the Constitution permits the trial judge, acting alone, to impose a capital sentence,... it is not offended when a State further requires a judge to consider a jury recommendation and trusts the judge to give it the proper weight....

CHAPTER III

LEGAL DECISIONS

CIRCUMSTANCES, RIGHT TO COUNSEL, EVIDENCE, AND VICTIM IMPACT STATEMENTS

RAPE AND KIDNAPING DO NOT WARRANT DEATH

In June 20, 1977, a 5-4 divided Supreme Court ruled in *Everheart v. Georgia* and *Coker v. Georgia* (433 US 584, 1977) that

> rape is without doubt deserving of serious punishment, but in terms of moral depravity and of the injury to the person and to the public, it does not involve the unjustified taking of human life.... The murderer kills; the rapist, if no more than that, does not. Life is over for the victim of the murderers; for the rape victim, life may not be nearly so happy as it was, but it is not over and normally is not beyond repair. We have the abiding conviction that the death penalty, which is unique in its severity and irrevocability,... is an excessive penalty for the rapist who, as such, does not take human life.

The court also held that kidnaping did not warrant the death penalty. This left only the taking of human life and treason (the death penalty for which *Everheart* raises serious questions) as justifiable grounds for the imposition of the death penalty.

MITIGATING CIRCUMSTANCES

Sandra Lockett was convicted for helping to plan and then driving the getaway car for a pawnshop robbery. Although it was unplanned, the owner of the pawnshop was murdered. Lockett also hid her accomplices in her home. Later, she was tried for the capital murder of the pawnshop owner. According to the death penalty statute, capital punishment had to be imposed on Lockett unless "(1) the victim induced or facilitated the offense; (2) it is unlikely that the offense would have been committed but for the fact that the offender was under duress, coercion, or strong provocation; or (3) the offense was primarily the product of the offender's psychosis or mental deficiency." Lockett was found guilty and sentenced to die.

She appealed, claiming that the Ohio law did not give "the sentencing judge a full opportunity to consider mitigating circumstances," but rather limited the judge to those three conditions. In July 1978, the Supreme Court, in *Lockett v. Ohio* (438 US 586), upheld Lockett's contention. Chief Justice Burger observed,

> A statute that prevents the sentencer in capital cases from giving independent mitigating weights to aspects of the defendant's character and record and to the circumstances of the offense proffered in mitigation creates the risk that the death penalty will be imposed in spite of factors that may call for a less severe penalty, and when the choice is between life and death, such risk is unacceptable and incompatible with the commands of the Eighth and Fourteenth Amendments.

Since the Ohio statute did not permit an adequate consideration of mitigating circumstances, that part of it was found unconstitutional.

A unanimous Supreme Court further emphasized in *Hitchcock v. Dugger* (481 US 393, 1987) that all mitigating circumstances had to be considered before the convicted murderer could be sentenced. A Florida judge had instructed the jury not to consider, and himself refused to consider, evidence of mitigating factors that were not specifically indicated in the Florida death penalty law. Writing for the Court, Justice Scalia stressed that a convicted person had the right "to present any and all relevant mitigating evidence that is available."

Mitigating Circumstances
Must Always Be Considered

The High Court has consistently upheld the position that all mitigating circumstances must be considered before a convicted murderer may be sentenced to death. In *Sumner v. Shuman* (483 us 66, 1987), a 6-3 divided court upheld a lower court decision which voided a Nevada law that required the death sentence for a prisoner serving a life term who was found guilty of first degree murder. In 1958, Raymond Shuman had been convicted of first degree murder committed during a robbery and sentenced to life imprisonment without possibility of parole. In 1975, Shuman was found guilty of the first degree murder of a fellow prisoner and sentenced to die under a Nevada law requiring the death penalty for prisoners convicted under these circumstances.

Shuman appealed his conviction, which was upheld by the Nevada Supreme Court, but reversed by the Federal District Court and the Federal Court of Appeals. Agreeing with the lower federal courts, the Supreme Court noted that in its earlier rulings it had not ruled on limited, specific instances, such as an inmate sentenced to life for murdering another inmate or a guard, and would now use this opportunity to do so. The majority noted that the mandatory Nevada law in no way allowed for individual circumstances. While involvement in a killing was enough to convict an individual of murder, "in some cases it may not be sufficient to render death an appropriate sentence." The prisoner might not have done the actual murder or might not have intended the killing. In addition, approximately 35 percent of those sentenced to life imprisonment were sentenced for offenses other than murder, "yet under the [Nevada] mandatory statute, all predicate life-term offenses are given the same weight — a weight that is deemed to outweigh any possible combination of mitigating circumstances."

The Court indicated that removing the mandatory law did not mean the state of Nevada could not sentence such a prisoner to death, only that they had to consider all the factors involved in the killing before they sentenced the person to die. Even in the limited case where the state is trying to use the death sentence to control a prisoner who has little to lose by killing another person, all mitigating circumstances must be considered before the death penalty is imposed.

NOT BEING AT THE
SCENE OF THE MURDER

On April 1, 1975, Thomas Kersey opened the back door of his home to find Sampson and Jeanette Armstrong requesting water for their "overheated car." When Kersey came out of the house, Armstrong grabbed him, pointed a gun at him, and asked his wife, Jeanette, to get money. Kersey called for his wife, who came out of the house with a gun and shot Jeanette Armstrong. The two Armstrongs then killed the Kerseys. Meanwhile, Earl Enmund was waiting by the road in the getaway car. Enmund was tried with Sampson Armstrong as an aider and abettor in the robbery-murder and sentenced to death.

In *Enmund v. Florida* (468 US 782, 1982), a 5-4 split Supreme Court ruled that, in this case, the death penalty was a "cruel and unusual punishment" which violated the Eighth and Fourteenth Amendments of the U.S. Constitution. The majority noted that only 9 of the 36 states which had capital punishment permitted its use on a criminal who was not actually present at the scene of the crime (except in the case where someone had paid a hitman to murder the victim). Furthermore, over the years, juries had tended not to sentence criminals to death who had not actually been at the scene of the crime. Certainly Enmund was guilty of planning and participating in a robbery, but murder had not been part of the plan. Since only 0.48 percent of robberies end in death, Enmund could not have expected that the death of the Kerseys would follow from the robbery attempt. The Court observed,

> We have no doubt that robbery is a serious crime deserving serious punishment. It is not, however, a crime "so grievous an affront to humanity that the only adequate response may be the penalty of death" [from *Gregg v. Georgia*]. It does not compare with murder, which does involve the unjustified taking of human life. Although it may be accompanied by another crime, [robbery] by definition does not include the death of or even the serious injury to another person. The murderer kills; the robber, if no more than that, does not. Life is over for the victim of the murderer; for the [robbery] victim life ... is not over and normally is not beyond repair.

The Supreme Court concluded,

> it is fundamental that "causing harm intentionally must be punished more severely than causing the same harm unintentionally." ... Enmund did not kill or intend to kill and thus his culpability is plainly different from that of the robbers who killed; yet the state treated them alike.... Enmund's criminal culpability must be limited to his participation in the robbery, and his punishment must be tailored to his personal responsibility and moral guilt. Putting Enmund to death to avenge two killings that he did not commit and had no intention of committing or causing does not measurably contribute to the retributive end of ensuring that the criminal gets his just deserts.

Writing for the minority, Justice O'Connor concluded that intent is a complex issue which is difficult to determine. It should be left to the judge and jury trying the accused to decide intent, not a federal court far removed from the actual trial.

Enmund Reviewed

In January 1986, a 5-4 divided Supreme Court, in *Cabana v. Bullock* (474 US 376) modified the *Enmund* decision, indicating that while *Enmund* had to be considered somewhere during the judicial process, the initial jury trying the accused did not necessarily have to consider the *Enmund* ruling. Crawford Bullock and a friend, Ricky Tucker, had been drinking at a bar. An acquaintance, Mark Dickson, offered them a ride home. During the drive they got into an argument over money Dickson supposedly owed Tucker. This eventually grew into a fight outside the car. Bullock held Dickson while Tucker hit Dickson in the face with a whiskey bottle and punched him. Dickson fell to the ground, Tucker picked up a concrete block and smashed Dickson's head, killing him. Tucker and Bullock disposed of the body, and Bullock kept Dickson's car. When police spotted Bullock driving the car the next day and arrested him, he confessed.

Under Mississippi law, a person involved in a robbery which results in murder may be convicted of capital murder regardless of "the defendant's own lack of intent that any killing take place." The jury never was asked to consider whether Bullock in fact killed, attempted to kill, or intended to kill, and Bullock was convicted and sentenced to death as an accomplice to the crime. During the appeals process, the Mississippi Supreme Court confirmed that Bullock had been an accomplice in the murder and found that "the evidence is overwhelming that appellant was an active participant in the assault and homicide upon Mark Dickson."

The Supreme Court of the United States ruled that while the jury had not been made aware of the issue of intent, the Mississippi Supreme Court had considered this question. Since *Enmund* did not require that the issue of intent be presented at the initial jury trial, only that it be considered at some time during the judicial process, the State of Mississippi had met that requirement.

The four dissenters claimed that it was difficult for any appeals court to determine intent from reading a typed transcript of a trial. It was important to see the accused and other involved individuals to help to determine who was telling the truth and who was not. This is why *Enmund* must be raised to the jury so they can consider the question of intent in light of what they have seen and heard directly.

A "Reckless Indifference to the Value of Human Life" Is Just as Bad as Pulling the Trigger

Gary Tison was a convicted criminal who had been sentenced to life imprisonment for murdering a prison guard during an escape. Tison's three sons, his wife, his brother, Joseph, and other relatives planned and carried out a prison escape in which Gary Tison and a fellow prisoner, Randy Greenawalt, also a convicted murderer, were freed from prison. The sons entered the prison with weapons hidden in a large ice chest. They armed their father and Greenawalt. During the escape, their car had a flat tire. They had already used the spare, so they flagged down a passing car.

The motorist who stopped to help was driving with his wife, their two-year-old child, and a 15-year-old niece. The escapees seized the family, and then drove their own car and their hostages' car into the desert. The Tisons switched their possessions into the family's car. Gary Tison then told his sons to go get some water from the motorist's car, presumably to be left with the hostages when they were left in the desert. While the sons were filling up water bottles, their father, Gary Tison, and Randy Greenawalt opened up on the hapless family with shotguns, killing them. Several days later two of the three brothers and Greenawalt were captured following a shootout. The third brother was killed, and the father escaped into the desert where he later died of exposure.

The captured Tison brothers and Greenawalt were found guilty and sentenced to death. The brothers, basing their claim on *Enmund*, appealed, claiming that they had neither pulled the triggers nor intended the deaths of the family that had stopped to help them. The 5-4 Supreme Court decision (*Tison v. Arizona*, 481 US 137, 1987), upheld the death sentence, indicating that the Tison brothers had shown a "reckless indifference to the value of human life [which] may be every bit as shocking to the moral sense as an 'intent to kill.'" The brothers knew that their father and Greenawalt were convicted murderers. They helped them escape from prison and helped them flag down the victims. They did nothing to help the victims before, during, or after the shootings. They continued to help the escapees until they were all captured or killed. "These facts," concluded Justice O'Connor for the majority, "not only indicate that the Tison brothers' participation in the crime was anything but minor, they also would clearly support a finding that they both subjectively appreciated that their acts were likely to result in the taking of innocent life."

The Tison brothers may not have pulled the triggers (and the Court fully accepted the premise that they did not do the shootings or directly intend them to happen), but they released and then assisted two convicted murderers. They should have realized that by helping these two killers to escape they could very well have been putting innocent people in extreme danger. Unlike the situation in the *Enmund* case, they were not sitting in a car far from the murder scene. They were direct participants in the whole event. The death sentence would stand.

Writing for the minority, Justice Brennan observed that had a prison guard been murdered (Gary Tison had murdered a prison guard in a previous escape attempt), then the Court's argument would have made sense. However, the murder of the family made no sense and was not even necessary for the escape. The Tison brothers were away from the murder scene and were, in fact, getting water for the victims, and could have done nothing to save them. While they were guilty of planning and carrying out an escape, the murder of the family who stopped to help them was an unexpected outcome of the escape. Furthermore, the father had promised his sons that he would not kill during the escape, a promise he had kept despite several opportunities to kill during the actual prison escape, so it was not unreasonable for the sons to not have expected him to kill in a situation that did not appear to warrant it. Justice Brennan concluded that "like Enmund, the Tisons neither killed nor attempted nor intended to kill anyone. Like Enmund, the Tisons have been sentenced to death for the intentional acts of others which the Tisons did not expect, which were not essential to the felony, and over which they had no control."

AN "OUTRAGEOUSLY OR WANTONLY VILE" MURDER?

Robert Godfrey separated from his wife of 28 years after a heated dispute. Mrs. Godfrey went to her mother, who supported her daughter's decision to leave her husband. Following an argument over the telephone during which Mrs. Godfrey declared that reconciliation was impossible, Mr. Godfrey took a shotgun and went to his mother-in-law's nearby trailer. He shot through a window, killing his wife instantly, went into the trailer, struck his fleeing daughter on the head with the gun, and then shot his mother-in-law in the head, killing her. Godfrey then called the police, told them what he had done, and sat down to wait for the police to arrive.

The Georgia Code permits the imposition of the death penalty in the case of a murder that "was outrageously or wantonly vile, horrible or inhuman in that it involved torture, depravity of mind, or an aggravated brutality to the victim. Aware of this law, the jury sentenced Godfrey to die. He appealed, claiming that the statute was unconstitutionally vague. The Georgia Supreme Court upheld the lower court, and the case was appealed to the Supreme Court.

The Supreme Court, in *Godfrey v. Georgia* (446 US 420, 1980), noted that in the past, the Georgia Supreme Court had been careful to uphold the death penalty in cases involving torture and abuse before the murder. However, the Supreme Court noted that in this case the "circumstances ... [did] not satisfy the criteria laid out by the Georgia Supreme Court itself." The Supreme Court noted that the victims were killed instantly (i.e., there was no torture), the victims had been "causing him extreme emotional trauma," and he acknowledged his responsibility. While this in no way, of course, excused the murders, the High Court could see "no principled way to distinguish this case, in which the death penalty was imposed, from the many cases in which it was not."

Consequently, the Court found that in this case the Georgia law was unconstitutionally vague. In a concurring opinion, Justice Marshall, with whom Justice Brennan joined, found this an example of the inherently "arbitrary and capricious" nature of capital punishment since even the prosecutor in Godfrey's case observed numerous times that there was no torture or abuse involved; yet, the Georgia Supreme Court chose to uphold the conviction without any attempt to narrow the definition of "outrageously or wantonly vile." Marshall, along with Brennan, concluded that

> even if the Court is unwilling to accept the view that the death penalty is so barbaric that it is in all circumstances cruel and unusual punishment forbidden by the Eighth and Fourteenth Amendments, it may eventually conclude that the effort to eliminate arbitrariness in the inflic- tion of that ultimate sanction is so

plainly doomed to failure that it —
and the death penalty — must be
abandoned altogether.

COMPARATIVE
PROPORTIONALITY REVIEW

Robert Harris and his brother decided to steal a car they would need for a getaway in a planned bank robbery. Robert Harris approached two teenage boys eating hamburgers in a car. He forced them at gunpoint to drive to a nearby wooded area. The teenagers offered to delay telling the police of the car robbery and even give the authorities misleading descriptions of the two robbers. When one of the boys appeared to be fleeing, Harris shot both of them. Harris and his brother later committed the robbery, were soon caught, and confessed to the robbery and murders.

Harris was found guilty. In California, a convicted murderer could only be sentenced to death or life imprisonment without parole if "special circumstances" existed and the murder had been "willful, deliberate, premeditated, and committed during the commission of kidnaping and robbery." This had to be proved during a separate sentencing hearing. The state showed that Harris had been convicted of manslaughter in 1975; he had been found in possession of a make-shift knife and garrote (instrument used for strangulation) while in prison; he and other inmates had sodomized another inmate; and he had threatened that inmate's life. Harris testified he had a very unhappy childhood, had little education, and his father had sexually molested his sisters. The jury sentenced Harris to death, and the judge refused to change their decision.

Harris claimed the U.S. Constitution, as interpreted in previous capital punishment rulings, required the State of California to give his case "comparative proportionality review" to determine if his death sentence was not out of line with others convicted of similar crimes. In "comparative proportionality review," a court considers the seriousness of the offense, the severity of the penalty, the sentences imposed for other crimes, and the sentencing in other jurisdictions for the same crime. Courts have occasionally struck down punishments inherently disproportionate and therefore cruel and unusual. Georgia, by law, and Florida, by practice, had incorporated such reviews in their procedures. Other states, such as Texas and California, had not.

After several appeals, the United States Ninth Circuit Court of Appeals agreed with Harris, and ordered California to establish proportionality or lift the death sentence. On appeal, the Supreme Court, in *Pulley v. Harris* (465 US 37, 1984) was "unimpressed" and, in a 7-2 decision, reversed the lower court's findings. Certainly Georgia and Florida's capital punishment procedures, which the High Court had approved, included "propor-tionality," but nowhere in *Coker v. Georgia* (428 US 584, 1977) had the Court found it to be necessary.

> That some schemes providing pro-portionality review are constitutional does not mean that such review is indispensable.... To endorse the statute as a whole is not to say that anything different is unacceptable. Examination of our 1976 cases makes clear that they do not establish proportionality review as a constitu-tional requirement.

The California procedure contained enough safeguards to guarantee a defendant a fair trial and those convicted a fair sentence. The High Court upheld Harris' death sentence.

Justice Brennan, joined by Justice Marshall, dissented. He noted the Supreme Court had thrown out the existing death penalty procedures during the 1970s because they were "arbitrary and capricious." He believed they still were, but the introduction of "proportionality" might "elimi-nate some, if only a small part, of the irrationality that currently surrounds the imposition of the death penalty."

WHEN DOES THE RIGHT
TO COUNSEL END?

The State of Virginia permitted condemned prisoners the right to use the prison libraries to prepare their appeals. "Unit attorneys" (attorneys assigned to the prison to help all prisoners with prison-related legal matters) were available to offer guidance to death row inmates, but they were in no way a personal attorney for any one particular inmate. Joseph Giarratano was a Virginia prisoner under sentence of death. He went to court, complaining that, because he was poor, the State of Virginia should be required to provide him with a lawyer to help prepare conviction appeals. Included among the defendants was Edward Murray, director of the Virginia Department of Corrections. This case became a class action in which the Federal District Court certified a class comprising "all current and future Virginia inmates awaiting execution who do not have and cannot afford counsel to pursue postconviction proceedings."

The Federal District Court and the Federal Court of Appeals agreed with Giarratano, but the U.S. Supreme Court, in *Murray v. Giarratano* (492 US 1, 1989), did not. Writing for the majority (Justices Rehnquist, White, O'Connor, and Scalia, with Justice Kennedy filing a concurring opinion), Chief Justice Rehnquist concluded that while the Sixth and Fourteenth Amendments of the U.S. Constitution assured an indigent (poor) defendant the right to counsel at the trial stage of a criminal proceeding, "there was no constitutional right to counsel for indigent prisoners seeking state postconviction relief."

Chief Justice Rehnquist agreed that those facing the death penalty had a right to counsel for the trial and during the initial appeal. During these periods, the defendant needed a heightened measure of protection, because the death penalty was involved. Later appeals, however, involved more procedural matters which "serve a different and more limited purpose than either the trial or appeal." The Supreme Court, in *Pennsylvania v.*

Finley (481 US 551, 1987), had ruled that "the Constitution did not require States to provide counsel in postconviction proceedings." The majority did not believe that, since *Pennsylvania v. Finley* had not specifically considered prisoners on death row, but all prisoners in general, the decision needed to be reconsidered because death-row prisoners had more at stake.

In *Bounds v. Smith* (430 US 817, 1977), the Supreme Court had "required a state to furnish access to adequate law libraries in order that the prisoners might prepare petitions for judicial relief." This the State of Virginia had done. Whether the time allotted for library services was sufficient was an issue to be debated in another case. Therefore, the U.S. Supreme Court reversed the findings of the lower federal courts. Justice Kennedy, in a concurring opinion, in which Justice O'Connor joined, observed,

> While Virginia has not adopted procedures for securing representation that are as far-reaching and effective as those available in other States, no prisoner on death row in Virginia has been unable to obtain counsel to represent him in postconviction proceedings and Virginia's prison system is staffed with institutional lawyers to assist in preparing petitions for post-conviction relief. I am not prepared to say that this scheme violates the Constitution.

In dissent, Justice Stevens (joined by Justices Brennan, Marshall, and Blackmun) indicated that he thought condemned prisoners in Virginia faced three critical differences from those considered in *Finley*. First, the Virginia prisoners had been sentenced to death, which makes their condition "quantitatively different from a sentence of imprisonment, however long." Second, Virginia's particular judicial decision forbids certain issues to be raised during the direct review or appeal process and forces them to be considered only during later postconviction appeals. This means that very important issues may be considered without the benefit of counsel. Finally,

> ... the death row inmate has an extremely limited period [of time] to prepare and present his postconviction petition and any necessary applications for stays of execution. Unlike the ordinary inmate, who presumably has ample time to use and reuse the prison library and to seek guidance from other prisoners experienced in preparing ... petitions, a grim deadline imposes a finite limit on the condemned person's capacity for useful research.... [As the District Court concluded,] an inmate preparing himself and his family for impending death is incapable of performing the mental functions necessary to adequately pursue his claims.

FEDERAL JUDGES CAN DELAY EXECUTIONS TO ALLOW *HABEAS* REVIEWS

A Texas jury found Frank McFarland guilty of stabbing to death a woman he had met in a bar. The Texas Appeals Courts upheld his conviction, and two lower federal courts refused his request for a stay of execution. The federal courts ruled they did not have jurisdiction to stop the execution until McFarland filed a *habeas* petition (state prisoner's method of getting heard in federal court). The inmate argued that without the stay, he would be executed before he could obtain a lawyer to prepare the petition.

The Supreme Court granted a stay of execution. In a 5-4 decision (*McFarland v. Scott* 114 S.Ct., 2568, 1994), the Supreme Court ruled that federal law required governments to supply lawyers for poor defendants on death row who wanted to have *habeas* review. Once a defendant requested counsel, the federal courts could postpone executions so the lawyers would have time to prepare an appeal. Justice Blackmun stated that "by providing indigent capital defendants with a mandatory right to qualified legal counsel in these proceedings, Congress has recognized that Federal *habeas corpus* has a particularly important role to play in promoting fundamental fairness in the imposition of the death penalty."

This case illustrated a problem in many states, particularly Texas, where there were 386 inmates on death row and 118 lawyers with the Texas Resource Center, a federally financed legal office that handled capital cases. In 1993, judges in Texas set 100 execution dates (state policy is that an execution must be scheduled about 45 days after the death sentence has been upheld on direct review). If McFarland had drafted his own *habeas* petition, it would probably have been rejected as inadequate, and due to recent court rulings, an inmate has only one chance at filing a federal *habeas* petition.

HARMLESS ERROR

Is Coerced Confession Harmless Error?

Oreste C. Fulminante called the Mesa, Arizona, police to report the disappearance of his 11-year-old stepdaughter, Jeneane Michelle Hunt. Fulminante was caring for the child while his wife, Jeneane's mother, was in the hospital. Several days later, Jeneane's body was found in the desert east of Mesa with two shots to the head, fired at close range by a large caliber weapon. There was a ligature (a cord used in tying or binding) around her neck. Because of the decomposed state of her body, it was not possible to determine whether she had been sexually assaulted.

Fulminante's statements about the child's disappearance and his relationship to her included inconsistencies that made him a suspect in her death. However, when he was not charged with the murder, Fulminante left Arizona for New Jersey where he was eventually convicted on federal charges of unlawful possession of a firearm by a felon.

While incarcerated, he became friendly with Anthony Sarivola, who was a former police officer who had been involved in loansharking for organized crime, but then became a paid informant for the Federal Bureau of Investigation (FBI). While imprisoned, he masqueraded as an organized crime figure. After befriending Fulminante, he heard a rumor that Fulminante was suspected of killing a child in Arizona. Initially, when questioned by Sarivola, Fulminante denied any involvement in his stepdaughter's murder. One time he said that Jeneane had been killed by bikers looking for drugs; on another occasion he said he had no idea what happened. When Sarivola told the FBI what Fulminante had said, the agency instructed him to find out more.

One evening Sarivola mentioned to Fulminante that he knew Fulminante was "starting to get some tough treatment and what not" from the other inmates because of the rumor about his involvement with his stepdaughter. Sarivola offered him protection from the other inmates, but only on the condition that, "You have to tell me about it ... [f]or me to give you any help." Fulminante admitted to Sarivola that he had taken Jeneane to the desert on his motorcycle, choked her, sexually assaulted her, made her beg for her life, and then shot her twice in the head.

Sarivola was released from prison the following month. Fulminante, released six months later, was arrested again within 30 days for another weapons violation. Fulminante was indicted in Arizona for the first degree murder of Jeneane. In a hearing prior to the trial, Fulminante moved to suppress (remove from the record) the statement he had made to Sarivola in prison and then later to Sarivola's wife, Donna, following his release from prison. He maintained that the confession to Sarivola was coerced, and that the second confession was the "fruit" of the first one. The trial court denied the motion to suppress, finding that, based on the specified facts, the confessions were voluntary. The state introduced both confessions as evidence at the trial; Fulminante was convicted of Jeneane's murder and subsequently sentenced to death.

In his appeal, Fulminante argued, among other things, that his confession to Sarivola was coerced and that its use at the trial violated his rights of due process under the Fifth and Fourteenth Amendments of the U.S. Constitution. The Arizona Supreme Court held the confession was coerced, but initially determined that the admission of the confession at the trial was a harmless error* because of the overpowering evidence against Fulminante.

However, after Fulminante motioned for reconsideration, the Arizona court ruled that the U.S. Supreme Court had set a precedent that precluded (halted) the use of harmless-error analysis in the case of a coerced confession. The Arizona court reversed the conviction and ordered that Fulminante be retried without the use of the confession to Sarivola. Because of differences in the state and federal courts over the admission of a coerced confession with regard to harmless-error analysis, the Supreme Court agreed to hear the case.

In *Arizona v. Oreste C. Fulminante* (59 LW 4235, 1991), Justice White, writing for the majority, stated that although the question is a close one, the Arizona Supreme Court was right in concluding that Fulminante's confession had been coerced. He further noted

> The Arizona Supreme Court found a
> credible threat of physical violence
> unless Fulminante confessed. Our
> cases have (found) ... that a finding of
> coercion need not depend upon
> actual violence by a government
> agent; a credible threat is sufficient.
> As we have said, "coercion can be

---

*The harmless-error standard, as stated in *Chapman v. California* (386 U.S. 18, 24, 1967), held that an error is harmless if it appears "beyond a reasonable doubt that the error complained of did not contribute to the verdict obtained."

mental as well as physical, and ... the blood of the accused is not the only hallmark of an unconstitutional inquisition." There was a credible threat of physical violence ... [so that] Fulminante's will was overborne in such a way as to render his confession a product of coercion.

White further argued that the State of Arizona had failed to meet its burden of establishing, beyond a reasonable doubt, that the admission of Fulminante's confession to Sarivola was harmless. He wrote

> A defendant's confession is like no other evidence. Indeed, "the defendant's own confession is probably the most probative [providing evidence] that can be admitted against him... [T]he admissions of a defendant come from the actor himself, the most knowledgeable and unimpeachable source of information about his past conduct. Certainly confessions have a profound impact on the jury, so much so that we may justifiably doubt its ability to put them out of mind even if told to do so." *(Bruton v. United States*, 391 U.S. at 139-140.)

The transcript of the Fulminante trial revealed that in order for the jury to reach a guilty verdict, both confessions would have to be believed since it was unlikely that the physical and circumstantial evidence alone would have been enough for a conviction. The jury might have believed that the two confessions reinforced and corroborated each other. The Court concluded by saying that it is impossible to say, beyond a reasonable doubt, that the judge, who during the sentencing process relied on evidence that could be found only in the two confessions, would have given the death sentence without the confessions. The Court ruled that Fulminante should be retried without admission of the confessions.

Presumption of Malice As Harmless Error

Dale Robert Yates and Henry Davis robbed a country store in Greenville County, South Carolina. When they entered the store, only the owner, Willie Wood, was present. Yates and Davis showed their weapons, ordered the owner to give them money from the cash register, and eventually received $3,000 in cash from him. Davis handed Yates the money and ordered Wood to lie across the counter. Wood, who had a pistol beneath his jacket, refused. Meanwhile, Yates was backing out of the store with his gun pointed at the owner. After being told to do so by Davis, Yates fired two shots. The first bullet caused flesh wounds in Wood; the second shot missed. Yates then jumped into the car and waited for Davis. When Davis did not appear, he drove off. Inside the store, although wounded, Wood pursued Davis. As the two struggled, Wood's mother came in and ran to help her son. During the struggle, Mrs. Wood was stabbed once in the chest and died at the scene. Wood then shot Davis five times, killing him instantly.

After Yates was arrested and charged with murder, his primary defense was that Mrs. Wood's death was not the probable natural consequence of the robbery he had planned with Davis. He claimed that he had brought the weapon only to induce the owner to give him the cash and that neither he nor Davis intended to kill anyone during the robbery.

The prosecutor's case for murder hinged on the agreement between Yates and Davis to commit an armed robbery, arguing that they planned to kill any witnesses, thereby making homicide a probable or natural result of the robbery. The prosecutor concluded, "[i]t makes no difference who actually struck the fatal blow, the hand of one is the hand of all."

In his instructions to the jury, the judge said,

> Malice is implied or presumed by the law from the willful, deliberate and intentional doing of an unlawful act

without any just cause or excuse. In its general signification, malice means the doing of a wrongful act, intentionally, without justification of excuse.... I tell you, also, that malice is implied or presumed from the use of a deadly weapon.

The judge continued to instruct the jury on the theory of accomplice liability. The jury returned guilty verdicts on the murder charge and on all other counts in the indictment. The South Carolina Supreme Court affirmed the conviction.

Yates petitioned the State Supreme Court, asserting that the jury charge that "malice is implied or presumed from the use of a deadly weapon" was an unconstitutional burden-shifting instruction. The case was twice reviewed by the South Carolina Supreme Court, which agreed that the jury instructions were unconstitutional, but that allowing the jury to presume malice was a harmless error. As in *Fulminante* (see previous case), the state court found that it was its duty to determine "whether it is beyond a reasonable doubt that the jury would have found it unnecessary to rely on the erroneous mandatory presumption regarding the element of malice." The state found that the jury did not have to rely on presumptions of malice because the fact that Davis "lunged" at Mrs. Wood and stabbed her were acts of malice.

The U.S. Supreme Court, in *Yates v. Evatt* (59 LW 4509, 1991), reversed the decisions of the South Carolina Supreme Court and remanded (ordered a new trial) the case. Justice Souter, writing for the Court, ruled that the State Supreme Court failed to apply the proper harmless-error standard as stated in *Chapman* (see footnote in *Fulminante*). Souter further stated that an error does "not contribute to a verdict" only if it is unimportant in relation to everything else the jury considered. In order to satisfy the reasonable doubt standard established by *Chapman,*

> ... it will not be enough that the jury considered evidence from which it could have come to the verdict without reliance on the presumption. Rather the issue under *Chapman* is whether the jury actually rested its verdict on evidence establishing the presumed fact beyond a reasonable doubt, independently of the presumption.

Souter concluded by stating that there was clear evidence of Davis's attempt to kill Wood because he could have left the store with Yates, but stayed to pursue Wood with a deadly weapon. The evidence that Davis intended to kill Mrs. Wood was not as clear. In addition, Yates testified that neither he nor Davis intended to kill anyone and the record shows that he heard a woman scream as he left the store, but did not attempt to return and kill her. The jury could have interpreted Yates's behavior to confirm his claim that he and Davis had not originally intended to kill anyone. Even the prosecutor, in summation, conceded that "it appeared [Mrs. Wood] tried to grab Mr. Davis." The only certainty is that Mrs. Wood joined the struggle and was stabbed in the course of it. She could have been killed inadvertently by Davis. The evidence of Davis's intent to kill Mrs. Wood was not clear.

DUE PROCESS AND NOTIFICATION OF THE DEATH PENALTY

Robert and Cheryl Bravence were beaten to death at their campsite near Santiam Creek, Idaho. Two brothers, Bryan Stuart and Mark Lankford, were charged with first-degree murder. At the arraignment, the trial judge advised Bryan Lankford that "the maximum punishment that you may receive if you are convicted on either of the two charges is imprisonment for life or death."

Following the arraignment, Bryan Lankford's attorney made a deal with the prosecutor to a plea bargain in which Bryan Lankford agreed to take two lie-detector tests. Although the results were somewhat unclear, they convinced the prosecutor that Lankford's older brother, Mark, was primarily responsible for the crimes and was the actual killer of both victims. Bryan Lankford's attorney and the prosecutor agreed on an indeterminate sentence with a 10-year minimum in exchange for a guilty plea, subject to commitment from the trial judge that he would impose that sentence. The judge refused to make such a commitment, and the case went to trial.

The judge refused to instruct the jury that a specific intent to kill was required to support a conviction of first-degree murder. The jury found Bryan Lankford guilty on both counts. The sentencing hearing was postponed until after Mark's trial. Before the sentencing trial, at Bryan Lankford's request, the trial judge sent an order requiring the state to notify the court and Lankford whether it would seek the death penalty, and if so, to file a statement of the aggravating circumstance on which the death penalty would be based. The state filed the response with the judge, in which it said it would *not* recommend the death penalty for either count of first degree murder for which Bryan Lankford had been convicted. Several proceedings followed, including Lankford's request for a new attorney, a motion for a new trial, a motion for continuance of the sentencing hearing. At none of the proceedings was there any mention that Lankford might receive the death penalty.

At the sentencing hearing, again there was no mention as the prosecutor offered no evidence for the death penalty, but recommended an indeterminate life sentence with a minimum of "somewhere between ten and 20 years." The trial judge indicated that he considered Lankford's testimony unbelievable and that the seriousness of the crime warranted more severe punishment than recommended by the state. He eventually sentenced Lankford to death.

Lankford appealed on several grounds, including the assertion that the trial judge violated the Constitution by failing to give notice that he intended to impose the death penalty in spite of the state's earlier notice that it would not seek the death penalty. The judge maintained that Idaho Code provided Lankford with sufficient notice and the fact that the prosecutor said he would not seek the death penalty had "no bearing on the adequacy of notice to petitioner [Lankford] that the death penalty might be sought." The Idaho Supreme Court affirmed the conviction and the judge's decision to seek the death penalty following the conviction.

Writing for the majority in *Bryan Stuart Lankford v. Idaho* (59 LW 4434, 1991), Justice Stevens reversed the Idaho Supreme Court ruling and remanded the case for a new trial. Stevens wrote that the Due Process Clause of the Fourteenth Amendment was violated because at the time of the sentencing hearing, Lankford and his counsel did not have adequate notice that the judge might sentence him to death. There was nothing in the record following the state's pre-sentencing order or before the judge's remarks at the end of the hearing to indicate that the judge was contemplating death as a sentence or to alert Lankford and his attorney that the real issue they would be debating would be the choice between life and death. Stevens noted that

> If the defense counsel had been notified that the trial judge was contemplating a death sentence based on five specific aggravating circumstances, presumably she would have advanced arguments that addressed these circumstances; however, she did not make these arguments because they were entirely inappropriate in a discussion about the length of the petitioner's possible incarceration.

Stevens further indicated that the trial judge's silence, in effect, hid the principal issues to be decided from Lankford and his attorney, as well as from the prosecutor.

In a dissenting opinion, Justice Scalia wrote that Lankford's due process rights were not violated because he knew that he had been convicted of first-degree murder, and Idaho Code clearly states that "every person guilty of murder of the first degree shall be punished by death or by imprisonment for life." At the arraignment, the trial judge told Lankford that he could receive either punishment (see above). Scalia further noted that, in Idaho, the death penalty statute places full responsibility for determining the sentence on the judge. He foresaw numerous problems resulting from this decision.

> ... it is clear that the death penalty remained at issue in the sentencing hearing, and there is no basis for the contention that the judge "misled" Lankford to think otherwise.... If defendants are no longer to be held to knowledge of the law, or if their unreasonable expectations are henceforth to be criteria of the process which is their due, the lawfulness and finality of no conviction or sentence can be assured. The defense created by the Court today will always be available, its success to be limited by factors we will presumably seek to identify in a series of future cases that will undertake the impossible task of explaining how much ignorance of the law, or how much unreasonableness of expectation, is too much.

EVIDENCE AND APPEALS

Newly Discovered Evidence
Does Not Stop Execution

On an evening in late September, 1981, the body of Texas Department of Public Safety Officer David Rucker was found lying beside his patrol car. He had been shot in the head. At about the same time, police officer Enrique Carrisalez saw a vehicle speeding away from the area where Rucker's body had been found. Carrisalez and his partner chased the vehicle and pulled it over. Carrisalez walked to the car. The driver opened his door and exchanged a few words with the police officer before firing at least one shot into Carrisalez's chest. The officer died nine days later. Leonel Torres Herrera was arrested a few days after the shootings and charged with capital murder. He was tried, found guilty of murdering Carrisalez in January 1982, and sentenced to death. In July 1982, he pleaded guilty to the murder of Rucker.

At the trial, Carrisalez's partner identified Herrera as the person who fired the gun. He also testified that there was only one person in the car. In a statement by Carrisalez before he died, he also identified Herrera. The speeding car belonged to Herrera's girlfriend, and Herrera had the car keys in his pocket when he was arrested. Splatters of blood on the car and on Herrera's clothes were the same type as Rucker's. Strands of hair found in the car also belonged to Rucker. Finally, a handwritten letter was found on Herrera when he was arrested which strongly implied that he had killed Rucker.

In 1992, 10 years after the initial trial, Herrera appealed to the federal courts, alleging that he was innocent of the murders of Rucker and Carrisalez and that his execution would violate the Eighth and Fourteen Amendments. He presented affidavits (sworn statements) claiming that he had not killed the officers, but that his now dead brother had. The brother's attorney, one of his cellmates, and a school friend all swore that the brother had killed the police officers. His son said that he had witnessed his father killing the men.

The case was appealed and the U.S. Supreme Court, in *Herrera v. Collins* (113 S.Ct. 853, 1993), in a 7-3 decision, ruled that executing Herrera would not violate the Eighth and Fourteenth Amendments. The High Court said that the appeals process does not judge guilt or innocence; the trial does that. Appeals courts only determine the fairness of the proceedings.

Writing for the majority, Chief Justice Rehnquist stated,

> A person when first charged with a crime is entitled to a presumption of innocence and may insist that his guilt be established beyond a

reasonable doubt.... Once a defendant has been afforded a fair trial and convicted of the offense for which he was charged, the presumption of innocence disappears.... Here, it is not disputed that the State met its burden of proving at trial that petitioner was guilty of the capital murder of Officer Carrisalez beyond a reasonable doubt. Thus, in the eyes of the law, petitioner does not come before the Court as one who is "innocent," but on the contrary as one who has been convicted by due process of two brutal murders.

Based on affidavits here filed, petitioner claims that evidence never presented to the trial court proves him innocent....

Claims of actual innocence based on newly discovered evidence have never been held to state a ground for [court] relief absent an independent constitutional violation occurring in the underlying state criminal proceeding....

This rule is grounded in the principle that ... [appeals] courts sit to ensure that individuals are not imprisoned in violation of the Constitution — not to correct errors of fact....

Rehnquist continued that states all allow the introduction of new evidence. Texas is one of 17 states that require a new trial motion based on new evidence within 60 days. Herrera's appeal came ten years later. However, the Chief Justice emphasized that Herrera still had options.

For under Texas law, petitioner may file a request for executive clemency. Executive clemency has provided the "fail safe" in our criminal justice system.... It is an unalterable fact that

our judicial system, like the human beings who administer it, is fallible. But history is replete with examples of wrongfully convicted persons who have been pardoned in the wake of after-discovered evidence establishing their innocence.

The majority opinion found the information presented in the affidavits inconsistent with the other evidence. The justices questioned why the affidavits were produced at the "eleventh hour," the last minute. The justices also wondered why Herrera had pleaded guilty to the murder of Rucker if he had been innocent. They did note that some of the information in the affidavits might have been important to the jury, "but coming 10 years after the ... trial, this showing of innocence falls far short of that which would have to be made in order to trigger the sort of constitutional claim [to decide for a retrial]." Concurring in the opinion, Justice O'Connor stated that "the record overwhelmingly demonstrates that petitioner deliberately shot and killed [the officers]." She wrote that the "affidavits pale when compared to the proof at trial."

Speaking for the minority, Justice Blackmun wrote,

We really are being asked to decide whether the Constitution forbids the execution of a person who has been validly convicted and sentenced but who, nonetheless, can prove his innocence with newly discovered evidence. Despite the State of Texas' astonishing protestation to the contrary,... I do not see how the answer can be anything but "yes."

The Eighth Amendment prohibits "cruel and unusual punishments." This proscription is not static but rather reflects evolving standards of decency. I think it is crystal clear that the execution of an innocent person is "at odds with contemporary standards of fairness and decency." ... The protection of the Eighth Amendment does not end once a defendant has been validly convicted and sentenced.

The Court also suggests that allowing petitioner to raise his claim of innocence would not serve society's interest in the reliable imposition of the death penalty because it might require a new trial that would be less accurate than the first. The question is not whether a second trial would be more reliable than the first but whether, in light of new evidence, the result of the first trial is sufficiently reliable for the State to carry out a death sentence....

The possibility of executive clemency is not sufficient to satisfy the requirements of the Eighth and Fourteenth Amendments. The majority correctly points out: "A pardon is an act of grace."

Miscarriage of Justice Claim

Lloyd Schlup, a Missouri prisoner, was convicted of participating in the murder of a fellow inmate and sentenced to death. He had filed one petition for *habeas corpus* (the means by which state prisoners get into federal court), arguing that he had inadequate counsel. He filed a second petition, alleging that constitutional error at his trial deprived the jury of crucial evidence that would have established his innocence. Under Supreme Court precedents, arguments not made in the first petition usually cannot be brought up in a second petition. Future petitions cannot be heard unless the prisoner shows that "a miscarriage of justice would result." The district court turned Schlup's petition down, using a previous Supreme Court ruling (*Sawyer v. Whitley*, 112 S.Ct. 2514, 1992), and saying that he had not shown "by clear and convincing evidence that but for a constitutional error, no reasonable juror would have found him guilty." Schlup's lawyers argued that the district court should have used another precedent (*Murray v. Carrier* 477 US 478, 1986), in which a petitioner need only to show that "a constitutional violation has probably resulted in the conviction of one who is actually innocent."

The Supreme Court differentiated this case (*Schlup v Delo*, 63 LW 4089, 1995) from *Herrera v. Collins* in that the former case involved an error-free trial, while Schlup's claim of innocence was

> accompanied by an assertion of constitutional error at trial: the ineffectiveness of his counsel and the withholding of evidence by the prosecution. As such, his conviction may not be entitled to the same degree of respect as one that is the product of an error-free trial, and his evidence of innocence need carry less of a burden....

The court further found that the "fundamental miscarriage of justice exception seeks to balance the societal interest in finality, and conservation of scarce judicial resources with the individual interest in justice that arises" in special cases. The justices thought that "claims of actual innocence pose less of a threat to scarce judicial resources, and to principle of finality ... than do claims that focus solely on the erroneous imposition of the death penalty." The court heard many cases challenging the death penalty; it rarely had cases of "a substantial claim that constitutional error has caused the conviction of an innocent person. To put forth such a claim, the petitioner must support his allegations of constitutional error with new reliable evidence." Because such evidence is obviously unavailable in most cases, claims of actual innocence are rarely successful.

The court continued that "the quintessential miscarriage of justice is the execution of a person who is entirely innocent." In hearing a petitioner, a district court must not use its independent judgement as to whether reasonable doubt exists;... rather the standard requires the district court to make a probabilistic determination about what reasonable, properly instructed jurors would do. Thus a petitioner does not meet the threshold requirement unless he persuades the district court that, in light of the new evidence, no juror, acting reasonably, would have voted to find him guilty beyond a reasonable doubt.

In Schlup's case, if the new evidence was true, then a juror "conscientiously following instructions could not have voted to convict. The statements, though, could have been unreliable, but that is not under the district court's consideration." The Supreme Court decided to send the case back to the Court of Appeals with instructions to send it back to the district court for "further proceedings consistent with this opinion."

Suppressed Evidence Means a New Trial

Curtis Lee Kyles was convicted of first-degree murder by a Louisiana jury and sentenced to death. It was revealed on review that the prosecutor had never disclosed certain evidence favorable to the defendant. The State Supreme Court, the federal district court, and the Fifth Circuit Court denied Kyles' appeals. The United States Supreme Court (*Kyles v. Whitley*, 63 LW 4303, 1995) reversed the lower courts' decisions.

The High Court ruled that, "favorable evidence is material, and constitutional error results from its suppression by the government, if there is a "reasonable probability" that, had the evidence been disclosed to the defense, the result of the proceeding would have been different." In this case, the Supreme Court found that the "net effect of the state-suppressed evidence favoring Kyles raises a reasonable probability that disclosure would have produced a different result

at trial." The conviction was overturned, and Kyles could have a new trial.

VICTIM IMPACT STATEMENTS

First, They Are Not Constitutional

John Booth and Willie Reid stole money from elderly neighbors to buy heroin. Booth, knowing his neighbors could identify him, tied up the elderly couple and then repeatedly stabbed them in the chest with a kitchen knife. The couple's son found their bodies two days later. Booth and Reid were found guilty.

The State of Maryland permitted a victim impact statement (VIS) to be read to the jury during the sentencing phase of the trial. The VIS prepared in this case explained the tremendous pain caused by the murder of their parents and grandparents to the family. It revealed that not only had the murdered victims suffered, but their family also suffered severely in many ways including sleepless nights, lack of trust, depression, disorientation, etc. A 5-4 Supreme Court, in *Booth v. Maryland* (482 US 496, 1987), while recognizing the agony caused to the victim's family, ruled that victim impact statements were unconstitutional and could not be used during the sentencing phase of a capital murder trial.

Writing for the majority, Justice Powell indicated that "a jury must make 'an individualized determination' of whether the defendant in question should be executed, based on 'the character of the individual and the circumstances of the crime.'" These factors have nothing to do with the victim. Furthermore, some families could express the pain and disruption they suffered as a result of the murder better than other families. Should a sentencing be dependent upon how well a family could express its grief? In addition, if the character of the victim should play a role in determining the sentence, then the prisoner should have the right to attack that character to show it was not as flawless as likely presented. This could likely lead to attacks on the character of the victim and more pain for the victim's family.

Finally, there is no "justification for permitting such a decision to turn on the perception that the victim was a sterling member of the community rather than someone of questionable character." The High Court was "troubled by the implication that defendants whose victims were assets to their community are more deserving of punishment than those whose victims are perceived to be less worthy. Of course, our system of justice does not tolerate such distinctions." It is the crime and the criminal that are at issue, declared the High Court. Had Booth and Reid viciously murdered a drunken bum, the crime would have been just as horrible.

Two years later, in *South Carolina v. Gathers* (490 US 805, 1989), the High Court, still divided 5-4, upheld *Booth*. Richard Haynes, a 31-year-old unemployed man with a history of mental problems, was sitting on a park bench. Mr. Haynes considered himself a religious man and carried several bags containing religious articles including two Bibles, rosary beads, plastic statues, and religious writings. Demetrius Gathers and three companions sat down on the bench next to Haynes. Haynes indicated that he did not want to talk to them. The four boys then beat up and kicked Haynes and smashed a bottle over his head. They left him alive, but Gathers returned later and finished the job by stabbing Haynes to death.

A jury found Gathers guilty. During the sentencing phase, the prosecutor noted all the religious items, which Gather and his companions had rifled to see if there was anything worth stealing, and stressed that the victim had been a very religious man. In addition, he noted Haynes had a voter registration card, showing that Haynes was civic-minded. Gathers appealed the death sentence to the South Carolina Supreme Court and the court reversed his sentence, concluding that the prosecutor's remarks "conveyed the suggestion appellant deserved a death sentence because the victim was a religious man and a registered voter." The U.S. Supreme Court, in *South Carolina v. Gathers,* agreed with the South Carolina court.

And Then They Are

Pervis Tyronne Payne spent the morning and early afternoon injecting cocaine and drinking beer. Later, he drove around the town with a friend, each of them taking turns reading a pornographic magazine. Around 3 P.M., Payne went to his girlfriend's apartment, which was across the hall from the apartment of Charisse Christopher. He entered the Christophers' apartment and made sexual advances toward Charisse, who resisted. Payne become violent. Hearing screams, a neighbor called the police. The first police officer to arrive at the scene saw Payne leaving the building so covered with blood that he appeared to be "sweating blood." Inside the apartment, the police saw Charisse and her children lying on the floor in the kitchen. Blood covered the walls and floor throughout the apartment. Charisse had 42 direct knife wounds and 42 defensive wounds on her arms and hands. The two-year-old daughter had suffered stab wounds to the chest, abdomen, back, and head. The murder weapon, a butcher knife, was found at her feet. Charisse's three-year old son, despite several wounds that went completely through his body, was still alive. Payne was arrested, and a Tennessee jury convicted Payne of the first-degree murders of Charisse Christopher and her daughter, and of first-degree assault, with intent to murder Charisse's son, Nicholas.

During the sentencing phase of the trial, Payne called his parents, his girlfriend, and a clinical psychologist to testify about the mitigating aspects of his background and character. The prosecutor, on the other hand, called Nicholas's grandmother, who testified how much the child missed his mother and baby sister. In arguing for the death penalty, the prosecutor commented on the continuing effects the crime had had on Nicholas and his family. The jury sentenced Payne to death on each of the murder counts. The state supreme court affirmed, rejecting Payne's claim that the admission of the grandmother's testimony and the state's closing argument violated his Eighth Amendment rights under *Booth v. Maryland*.

On hearing the appeal (*Payne v Tennessee,* 111 S.Ct 2597, 1991), a 6-3 U.S. Supreme Court upheld the death penalty and overturned both *Booth* and *Gathers*. The Court ruled that the Eighth Amendment does not prohibit a jury from considering, at the sentencing phase of a capital trial, "victim impact" evidence relating to a victim's personal characteristics and the emotional impact of the murder on the victim's family. The Eighth Amendment also does not bar a prosecutor from arguing such evidence at the sentencing phase.

The Court reasoned that the assessment of harm caused by a defendant as a result of a crime has long been an important concern of criminal law in determining both the elements of the offense and the appropriate punishment. Victim impact evidence is simply another form or method of informing the sentencing jury or judge about the specific harm caused by the crime in question. The *Booth* case unfairly weighted the scales in a capital trial. While virtually no limits were placed on the relevant mitigating evidence a capital defendant might introduce concerning his own circumstances, the state was barred from either offering a glimpse of the life which a defendant chose to extinguish or showing the loss to the victim's family or to society. *Booth* and *Gathers* were decided by narrow margins, the Court continued, and have been questioned by members of the Supreme Court as well as the lower courts.

Chief Justice Rehnquist, delivering the opinion of the Court, stated

> ... "The State has a legitimate interest in counteracting the mitigating evidence which the defendant is entitled to put in, by reminding the sentencer that just as the murderer should be considered as an individual, so too the victim is an individual whose death represents a unique loss to society and in particular to his family." ...

... there is nothing unfair about allowing the jury to bear in mind that harm at the same time as it considers the mitigating evidence introduced by the defendant.

We thus hold that if the State chooses to permit the admission of criminal impact evidence and prosecutorial argument on that subject, the Eighth Amendment erects no *per se* bar. A State may legitimately conclude that evidence about the victim and about the impact of the murder on the victim's family is relevant to the jury's decision as to whether or not the death penalty should be imposed. There is no reason to treat such evidence differently than other relevant evidence is treated.

Justice Stevens, dissenting, stated that a victim impact statement

> sheds no light on the defendant's guilt or moral culpability and thus serves no purpose other than to encourage jurors to decide in favor of death rather than life on the basis of their emotions rather than their reason....
>
> Victim impact evidence, as used in this case, has two flaws. First, aspects of the character of the victim, unforeseeable to the defendant at the time of his crime are irrelevant to the defendant's "personal responsibility and moral guilt" and therefore cannot justify a death sentence....
>
> Second, the quantity and quality of victim impact evidence sufficient to turn a verdict of life in prison into a verdict of death is not defined until after the crime has been committed and therefore cannot possibly be applied consistently in different cases.

CHAPTER IV

LEGAL DECISIONS
YOUTH, SANITY, RACE, AND METHODS OF EXECUTION

CAN A MINOR BE SENTENCED TO DEATH?

Perhaps*

Upon being pulled over by a police officer, Monty Lee Eddings told his companions that if the "mother ... pig tried to stop him he was going to blow him away." Eddings carried out the threat, was convicted of first-degree murder for killing a police officer, and was sentenced to death. At the time of the murder, he was 16 years old, but he was nonetheless tried as an adult. At the sentencing hearing following the conviction, Eddings' lawyer presented substantial evidence of a turbulent family history, beatings by a harsh father, and serious emotional disturbance. The judge refused, as a matter of law, to consider in mitigation the circumstances of the petitioner's unhappy upbringing and emotional disturbance and found that the only mitigating circumstance was the petitioner's youth, which was held to be insufficient to outweigh the aggravating circumstances.

Referring to *Lockett v. Ohio* (see Chapter III*)*, the Supreme Court, in a 5-4 opinion in *Eddings v. Oklahoma* (455 US 104, 1982), ordered the sentence vacated (thrown over) because nothing could or should be precluded as a matter of law from consideration as a mitigating factor. After consideration, such factors could be dismissed as insufficient, but all mitigating circumstances had to be considered. By implication, since the majority did not reverse the case on the issue of age, it let stand Oklahoma's decision to try him as an adult. Meanwhile, the dissenters, led by Chief Justice Burger, who filed the dissenting opinion in which Justices White, Blackmun, and Rehnquist joined, indicated that "there comes a time in every case when a court must 'bite the bullet'." The Chief Justice observed that

> The court stops far short of suggesting that there is any constitutional proscription against imposition of the death penalty on a person who was under age 18 when the murder was committed.

Hence, while the High Court did not directly rule on the question of minors being sentenced to death, the sense of the court would appear to be that it would uphold such a sentencing.

Not at Fifteen Years Old

William Thompson, along with three adults, brutally murdered a former brother-in-law whom they believed had abused their sister when he was married to her. They shot, knifed, beat, and kicked the victim. After chaining the body to a concrete block, they tossed it into the river. William Thompson was an active participant in the murder.

---

*In 1957, the United Nations adopted the International Covenant on Civil and Political Rights which forbids the execution of those under 18 years old. See Chapter IX.

Since Thompson was a juvenile of 15 at the time of the murder, the district attorney initiated a procedure to have Thompson tried as an adult. As part of the process, the court determined that in the case of Thompson, who had a long history of violent assault, there were "virtually no *reasonable* prospects for rehabilitation ... within the juvenile system and that [Thompson] should be held accountable for his acts as if he were an adult and should be certified to stand trial as an adult." William Thompson was tried as an adult and found guilty. As required by *Eddings* (see above), his age was considered a mitigating circumstance, but the jury still sentenced him to death.

Thompson appealed, and while the Court of Criminal Appeals of Oklahoma upheld the decision, the U.S. Supreme Court, in *Thompson v. Oklahoma* (487 US 815, 1988), did not. In a 5-3 majority vote, with Justice O'Connor agreeing to vacate the sentence, but not agreeing in the majority reasoning, the case was reversed. (Justice Kennedy took no part in the decision.) Writing for the majority (Justices Stevens, Brennan, Marshall, and Blackmun), Justice Stevens concluded that the decision should be based on "evolving standards of decency that mark the progress of a maturing society," a basis used in many other decisions.

Justice Stevens observed that

> Inexperience, less education, and less intelligence make the teenager less able to evaluate the consequences of his or her conduct while at the same time he or she is much more apt to be motivated by mere emotion or peer pressure than is an adult. The reasons why juveniles are not trusted with the privileges and responsibilities of an adult also explain why their irresponsible conduct is not as morally reprehensible as that of an adult.

Justice Stevens noted that 18 states required an age of at least 16 years before the death penalty could be considered. When this number was added to the 14 states prohibiting capital punishment, a majority of states did not execute people under 16 years of age. He further observed that only 18 to 20 such juveniles had been executed during the twentieth century, the last in 1948. Of the 1,393 persons sentenced to death between 1982 and 1986, only five were under 16 years of age. Even the Soviet Union prohibited juvenile executions, leading the majority to conclude that "it would offend civilized standards of decency to execute a person who was less than 16 years old" at the time the crime was committed. Based on these findings, Justice Stevens concluded that "contemporary standards, as reflected by the actions of legislatures and juries" had established that the execution of minors who had committed a murder while less than 16 years old was no longer acceptable.

Justice O'Connor thought that the decision should be reversed, but

> Although I believe that a national consensus forbidding the execution of any person for a crime committed before the age of 16 very likely does exist, I am reluctant to adopt this conclusion as a matter of constitutional law without better evidence than we now possess.

Justice O'Connor wondered whether just because most people of 15 are less blameworthy, some may well fully understand the horrible deed which they have done. The Justice would like to see the Oklahoma legislature carefully consider and debate the issue of executing minors who had committed crimes when less than 16 years old. If they did so and ruled that it was, indeed, the state's intent to execute minors, then she would accept that decision.

Writing for the minority (Justices Scalia, Rehnquist, and White), Justice Scalia found no national consensus that the execution of a person who had been 16 when the murder was committed was unacceptable. This child was not railroaded through the system. A careful hearing had considered his case. The fact that fewer and fewer young people were being executed reflected both the fact that fewer people, overall, were being executed and a reluctance, but not a prohibition, to give younger people the death sentence.

Justice Scalia could not understand the majority's calculations establishing a "contemporary standard" that no longer permitted the execution of young minors. On what basis did they combine the 18 states that prohibited the execution of those who were under the age of 16 when they murdered with the 14 states that banned the death penalty, and then count them altogether in order to get a majority? Abolitionist states should not be considered in the issue of executing minors since they do not consider executing anyone. Rather, they should be compared to the states that do have the death penalty, the 19 states "that have determined that no minimum age for capital punishment is appropriate, leaving that to be governed by their general rules for the age at which juveniles can be criminally responsible."

> When the Federal Government, and almost 40% of the States, including a majority of the States that include capital punishment as a permissible sanction, allow for the imposition of the death penalty on any juvenile who has been tried as an adult, which category can include juveniles under 16 at the time of the offense, it is obviously impossible for the plurality to rely upon any evolved societal consensus discernible in legislation — or at least discernible in the legislation of *this* society, which is assuredly all that is relevant.

In addition to finding no national consensus on this issue, Justice Scalia could find little basis for Justice O'Connor's suggestion that the Oklahoma legislature specifically consider the issue. "Is there any other group that needs to be specifically considered?" wondered Justice Scalia.

> If 15-year-olds must be explicitly named in capital statutes, why not those of extremely low intelligence, or those over 75, or any number of other appealing groups as to which the existence of a national consensus regarding capital punishment may be in doubt....

But It May Be Done at 16

While a majority of the court, with Justice O'Connor straddling the fence, found the age of 15 unacceptable, a majority of the Court found the ages of 16 and 17 acceptable. The Supreme Court, in two jointly considered cases, *Stanford v. Kentucky* and *Wilkins v. Missouri* (492 US 361, 1989), ruled that juveniles of 16 and 17 could be executed for murder.

When he was 17 years old, Kevin Stanford and an accomplice repeatedly raped and sodomized (anal intercourse) Baerbel Moore, the attendant at a gas station they were robbing. They then took Ms. Moore to a secluded area near the station, where Stanford shot her point-blank in the face and then in the back of her head. Stressing the seriousness of the offense and Stanford's long history of juvenile delinquency, the juvenile court certified him as an adult. He was tried, found guilty, and sentenced to death.

When he was 16 years old, Heath Wilkins stabbed Nancy Allen to death while he was robbing the convenience store where she worked. He stabbed her three different times while he was robbing the store. Wilkins indicated that he had fully intended to kill whomever was behind the counter at the convenience store because "a dead person can't talk." Based on his long history of juvenile delinquency, the court ordered Wilkins tried as an adult. He was found guilty and sentenced to die.

Writing for the majority (Justices Scalia, Rehnquist, White, and Kennedy), Justice Scalia could find no national consensus against executing minors of the age of 16 and 17. "Of the 37 States whose laws permit capital punishment, 15 decline to impose it on 17-year-old offenders. This does not establish the degree of national consensus this Court has previously thought sufficient to label a particular punishment cruel and unusual."

Justice Scalia saw no connection between the fact that those under 18 years old were denied the right to drink or vote and the question of whether a minor was "mature enough to understand that murdering another human being is profoundly wrong, and to conform one's conduct to that most minimal of all civilized standards." Justice Scalia concluded that

> The audience for these arguments, in other words, is not this Court but the citizenry of the United States. It is they, not we, who must be persuaded. Our job is to *identify* the "evolving standards of decency"; to determine, not what they *should* be, but what they *are*. We have no power under the Eighth Amendment to substitute our belief in the scientific evidence for the society's apparent skepticism. In short, we emphatically reject petitioner's suggestion that the issues in this case permit us to apply our "own informed judgment" ... regarding the desirability of permitting the death penalty for crimes by 16- and 17-year-olds.

Justice O'Connor, citing her earlier observations in *Thompson v. Oklahoma* (see above), indicated that

> Applying the same standard today, I conclude that the death sentences for capital murder imposed by Missouri and Kentucky on petitioners Wilkins and Stanford should not be set aside because it is sufficiently clear that no national consensus forbids the impo-

sition of capital punishment on 16 or 17-year-old capital murderers.

Furthermore, Kentucky specified 16 as the minimum age, and Missouri's legislature had considered the issue of the death penalty for minors of the defendants' ages.

Now writing for the minority (Justices Brennan, Marshall, Blackmun, and Stevens), Justice Brennan found a national consensus when he added to the 12 states forbidding the execution of a minor of 16 years to those states with no capital punishment and the states that, in practice, did not execute minors, a total of "30 states [that] would not permit Wilkin's execution." Justice Brennan further found that "adolescent offenders make up only a small proportion of the current death row population: 30 out of a total of 2,186 inmates, or 1.37 percent" which surely made such a sentence "unusual."

Justice Brennan took serious exception to the majority's observation that they had to find a national consensus in the laws passed by the state legislatures.

> Our judgment about the constitutionality of a punishment under the Eighth Amendment is informed, though not determined ... by an examination of contemporary attitudes toward the punishment, as evidenced in the actions of legislatures and of juries. The views of organizations with expertise in relevant fields and the choices of governments elsewhere in the world also merit our attention as indicators whether a punishment is acceptable in a civilized society.

Justice Brennan thought the very purpose of the Bill of Rights was to "withdraw certain subjects from the vicissitudes [unpredictable changes] of political controversy." Our Founding Fathers, Justice Brennan claimed, did not mean the Bill of Rights to be decided by a vote of the majority. While state legislation must be considered, the final decision "must be decided on the basis of our own judgment in the light of the precedents of this Court."

Consequently, Justice Brennan cited more than two dozen briefs from organizations opposing the execution of minors, including the American Bar Association, the Children's Defense Fund, the American Baptist Church, and the United States Catholic Conference. Furthermore, he stated that the overwhelming majority of nations did not execute minors. Since 1979, only the United States, Pakistan, Bangladesh, Rwanda, and Barbados had executed people under 18 years of age.

Finally, the justice felt that juveniles are too immature to be completely responsible for their actions in the way that adults are held accountable. He believed society also holds this belief since it forbids juveniles to vote, drink, or serve on a jury and generally does not let them drive or get married without parental permission.

Youth — A Mitigating Circumstance

Dorsie Lee Johnson, Jr., age 19, with his companion Amanda Miles, robbed a convenience store in Snyder, Texas. They agreed that there should be no witnesses to the crime. After staking out the store, they found that the only employee during the predawn hours was a clerk, Jack Huddleston. They left the store to return later. After waiting for other customers to leave, they informed Huddleston that the store was being robbed and ordered him to lie on the floor. Huddleston complied and placed his hands behind his head. Johnson then shot him in the back of the neck, killing him. Miles emptied the cash registers of $160; they each grabbed a carton of cigarettes and fled.

The following month, Johnson was arrested in Colorado City, Texas, for a subsequent robbery and attempted murder of a store clerk. He confessed to the murder of Jack Huddleston and the robbery of the convenience store. During the selection of the jury, the defense attorneys asked potential jurors whether they believed that people were capable of change and whether they, the potential jurors, had ever done things as youth that they would not do now.

The only witness the defense called was Johnson's father, who told of his son's drug use, grief over the death of his mother two years before the crime, and the murder of his sister the following year. He especially talked of his son's youth and the fact that at age 19 he did not evaluate things the way a person of 30 or 35 would. Johnson was tried and convicted of capital murder. Under Texas law the homicide qualified as a capital offense because Johnson intentionally or knowingly caused Huddleston's death, and the murder was carried out in the course of committing a robbery.

After the jury found the defendant guilty of capital murder, a separate punishment phase was conducted to determine the sentence. Consistent with Texas law, the trial judge instructed the jury to answer two special issues: (1) whether Johnson's actions were committed deliberately and with the reasonable expectation that death would occur, and (2) whether there was a probability that he would commit further criminal acts of violence that would make him a continuing threat to society. The judge also clearly informed the jury that if it answered "yes" to both issues, the defendant would be sentenced to death. If the jury returned a "no" answer to either issue, the defendant would be sentenced to life in prison. The jury was not to consider or discuss the possibility of parole.

Of equal importance was the instruction that the jury could consider all the evidence submitted to it, both aggravating and mitigating (extenuating, justifying), in either phase of the trial. The jury unanimously answered yes to both special issues, and the trial court sentenced Johnson to death, as required by Texas law. The state appellate court denied Johnson's motions for a rehearing, which were based on seven allegations of error, none of which involved the instructions to the jury during the punishment phase of trial. Five days after the state court ruling, the U.S. Supreme Court issued its opinion in *Penry v. Lynaugh* (492 U.S. 302, 1989) (see below). Based on the *Penry* ruling, Johnson claimed that a separate instruction should have been given to the jury that would have allowed them to consider his youth. Again, the Court of Criminal Appeals rejected the petition.

Affirming the Texas appellate court decision, Justice Kennedy, delivering the opinion of the Court in *Dorsie Lee Johnson, Jr. v. Texas* (61 LW 4738, 1993), was joined by Justices Rehnquist, White, Scalia, and Thomas. Kennedy noted that the Texas special issues system allowed for adequate consideration of Johnson's youth and that there was no reasonable likelihood that the jury was denied the opportunity to consider the relevant aspects of his youth since it received the second special issue (see above) and was told to consider all mitigating evidence. He further stated that

> Even on a cold record, one cannot be unmoved by the testimony of petitioner's father urging that his son's actions were due in large part to his youth. It strains credulity to suppose that the jury would have viewed the evidence of petitioner's youth as outside its effective reach in answering the second special issue. The relevance of youth as a mitigating factor derives from the fact that the signature qualities of youth are transient; as individuals mature, the impetuousness and recklessness that may dominate in younger years can subside.... As long as the mitigating evidence is within "the effective reach of the sentencer," the requirements of the Eighth Amendment are satisfied.

Justice O'Connor, joined by Justices Blackmun, Stevens, and Souter, issued a dissenting opinion, in which she stated that the jurors were not allowed to give "full effect to his strongest mitigating circumstance: his youth." Hearing of his less than exemplary youth, a jury might easily conclude, as Johnson's did, that he would "constitute a continuing threat to society." While it was possible that the jury thought Johnson might outgrow his temper and violent behavior with maturity, it is more likely that the jury saw the pattern of escalating violence as an indication that Johnson would grow more violent with age. Even if the jurors saw Johnson's violence as transient, the dangerous behavior associated with that youth would not disappear for some time. However, O'Connor added,

> But even if the jury could give some mitigating effect to youth under the second special issue, the Constitution still would require an additional instruction in this case.... [It] would be required because not one of the special issues under the former Texas scheme ... allows a jury to give effect to the most relevant mitigating aspect of youth: its relation to a defendant's "culpability for the crime he committed." A violent and troubled young person may or may not grow up to be a violent and troubled adult, but what happens in the future is unrelated to the *culpability* of the defendant at the time he committed the crime.... A jury could conclude that a young person acted "deliberately" and that he will be dangerous in the future, yet still believe that he was less culpable *because of his youth* than an adult.

ROLE OF PSYCHIATRISTS

Is the Testimony of a Psychiatrist Valid?

In *Barefoot v. Estelle, Director, Texas Department of Corrections* (463 US 880, 1983) the High Court again ruled that local juries were in the best position to make decisions in deciding guilt and sentencing. In 1978, Thomas Barefoot was convicted of murdering a police officer and, in a separate sentencing trial, was condemned to death. His conviction and sentence were appealed numerous times and, in 1983, his case was argued before the U.S. Supreme Court. Among the issues debated was the validity of the testimony of psychiatrists and whether it was necessary for the psychiatrists to have interviewed Barefoot or was it enough for them to answer hypothetical questions which pertained to a hypothetical individual who acted like Barefoot.

During the sentencing phase of Barefoot's trial, two psychiatrists were put on the stand by the prosecution. Neither psychiatrist had actually interviewed Barefoot nor did either ask to do so. Both psychiatrists agreed that an individual with Barefoot's background and who had acted as Barefoot had in murdering the policeman represented a future threat to society. Partially based on this testimony, the sentencing jury sentenced Barefoot to death. Barefoot's attorneys claimed that psychiatrists, "individually and as a group, are incompetent to predict with an acceptable degree of reliability that a particular criminal will commit other crimes in the future and so represent a danger to the community." The plaintiff's lawyers also noted that, "in any event, psychiatrists should not be permitted to testify about future dangerousness in response to hypothetical questions and without having examined the defendant personally," and, furthermore, that psychiatric testimony was so unreliable as to be virtually worthless in determining the future possibility of criminal action. The split 6-3 Court rejected these arguments.

Referring to *Jurek v. Texas* (428 US 262, 1976, see Chapter I), an earlier case that, among other things, upheld the testimony of lay persons as to a convicted murderer's possible future actions, the court looked upon psychiatrists as just another group of people presenting testimony which the jury must consider. Like all evidence presented to the jury, a psychiatric observation

> should be admitted and its weight left
> to the fact finder, who would have the

benefit of cross examination and contrary evidence by the opposing party. Psychiatric testimony predicting dangerousness may be countered not only as erroneous in a particular case but as generally so unreliable that it should be ignored. If the jury may make up its mind about future dangerousness unaided by psychiatric testimony, jurors should not be barred from hearing the views of the State's psychiatrists along with opposing views of the defendant's doctors.

The court dismissed the arguments in the *amicus* brief (a friend-of-the-court brief prepared to enlighten the court) presented by the American Psychiatric Association (APA). The APA had indicated that psychiatric testimony was "almost entirely unreliable" in determining future actions and should not be considered in determining whether the death penalty should be imposed. The court claimed that while experts differed on this issue, such testimony had been traditionally accepted and that if the APA felt so adamantly about the issue, they should produce witnesses to counter the testimony of psychiatrists who believed that future actions could be reliably predicted. The Supreme Court concluded that such arguments were founded "on the premise that a jury will not be able to separate the wheat from the chaff. We do not share in this low evaluation of the adversary process."

The High Court also dismissed Barefoot's contention that the doctors needed to personally interview him. Such methods of observation and conclusion were quite normal in courtroom procedure and the psychiatric observations had been based on established facts. Barefoot's appeal was denied.

Justice Blackmun strongly dissented to the majority decision. He stated that

> The Court holds that psychiatric
> testimony about a defendant's future

dangerousness is admissible, despite the fact that such testimony is wrong two times out of three [according to the APA]. The Court reaches this result — even in a capital case — because, it is said, the testimony is subject to cross-examination and impeachment. In the present state of psychiatric knowledge, this is too much for me. One may accept this in a routine lawsuit for money damages, but when a person's life is at stake — no matter how heinous his offense — a requirement of greater reliability should prevail. In a capital case, the specious testimony of a psychiatrist, colored in the eyes of an impressionable jury by the inevitable untouchability of a medical specialist's words, equates with death itself.

Justice Blackmun emphasized that the weight of supposedly scientific-based testimony would have much greater influence upon a jury than that of a layperson who did not claim any medical or scientific degrees. This tendency to give greater credence to "scientific experts," despite the questionability of their "science," would be most difficult to overcome. "One can only wonder," wrote Justice Blackmun, "how juries are to separate valid from invalid expert opinions when the 'experts' themselves are so obviously unable to do so." The justice concluded that

> Surely, this Court's commitment to ensuring that death sentences are imposed reliably and reasonably requires that nonprobative and highly prejudicial testimony on the ultimate question of life or death be excluded from a capital sentencing hearing.... Ultimately, when the Court knows full well that psychiatrists' predictions of dangerousness are specious, there can be no excuse for imposing on the defendant, on pain of his life, the heavy burden of convincing a jury of laymen of the fraud.

A Prisoner Maintains Rights Before a Psychiatrist

During the commission of a robbery, Ernest Smith's accomplice fatally shot a grocery clerk (Smith had tried to shoot the clerk, but his weapon had jammed). The State of Texas indicated that it would seek the death penalty. Thereafter, the judge ordered the state's attorney to arrange a psychiatric examination of Smith by Dr. James Grigson to determine if Smith was competent to stand trial. Dr. Grigson interviewed Smith in jail for about 90 minutes and found him competent to stand trial.

Grigson had not obtained permission from Smith's attorneys to examine, had discussed his conclusions and diagnosis with the state's attorney, and had been told five days before the sentencing hearing that his testimony would be needed during the sentencing phase of the trial. Smith was found guilty, and during the sentencing phase of the trial, over the protests of the defendant's lawyers, Grigson testified that Smith was a "very severe sociopath;" that he would continue his previous behavior, which would "only get worse;" that he had no "regard for another human being's property or for their life;" that there was "no treatment, no medicine ... that in any way at all" would help him change; that he would commit similar crimes in the future; and that he had "no remorse or sorrow for what he has done." The jury sentenced Smith to death.

Smith appealed his sentencing, claiming he had not been informed of his rights, and both the Federal District Court and the U.S. Court of Appeals agreed. So did a unanimous 9-0 Supreme Court. The High Court, in *Estelle v. Smith* (451 US 454, 1981), concluded that "given the gravity of the decision to be made at the penalty phase, the State is not relieved of the obligation to observe fundamental constitutional guarantees." While the trial court had the right to determine if Smith was capable of standing trial, they had no right to use the information gathered against him during the sentencing phase without having first warned him of his Fifth Amendment rights. Noting *Miranda v. Arizona* (384 US 436, 1966), the Court continued,

> the Fifth Amendment privilege is available outside of criminal court proceedings and serves to protect persons in all settings in which their freedom of action is curtailed in any significant way from being compelled to incriminate themselves.... the prosecution may not use statements, whether exculpatory [to declare innocence] or inculpatory [to incriminate], stemming from custodial interrogation of the defendant unless it demonstrates the use of procedural safeguards effective to secure the privilege against self-incrimination.

Grigson had, in no way warned Smith that his testimony could be used against him in a situation that could cost him his life. The Constitution guaranteed Smith that right, so the Supreme Court overturned the sentence.

In a similar case involving Dr. Grigson, another unanimous Supreme Court (8-0, with Justice Kennedy taking no part in the decision), in *Satterwhite v. Texas* (486 US 249, 1988), ruled that the defendant had to be warned of his Constitutional rights. John Satterwhite was charged with murder committed during a robbery. Before Satterwhite was given counsel, the judge granted the state's request for a psychological examination to determine if Satterwhite was competent to stand trial. Satterwhite's attorney was not informed of this. He was examined by two psychologists. The district attorney requested a second psychiatric evaluation, which was granted, and again Satterwhite's defense attorney was not informed. The defendant was again examined by the same two psychologists.

It was a surprise to both the court and the defense that a letter to the trial court from psychiatrist James Grigson appeared in the court file. He apparently had also interviewed Satterwhite. Satterwhite was convicted and, over defense counsel's objections, the state produced Dr. Grigson, who testified that the defendant presented a continuing threat to society through acts of criminal violence. Satterwhite was sentenced to death.

Satterwhite appealed the sentence, claiming he had been denied his Sixth Amendment right to counsel. The Texas Court of Criminal Appeals agreed but concluded that the error was harmless because an average jury would have found the properly admitted evidence enough to sentence Satterwhite to death. The Supreme Court did not find these violations harmless. "Some constitutional violations … by their very nature cast so much doubt on the fairness of the trial process that, as a matter of law, they can never be considered harmless." This was certainly one of them.

Grigson had testified that on a scale of one to ten — where "ones" were mild sociopaths and "tens" were individuals with complete disregard for human life — Satterwhite was a "ten plus." Grigson had concluded his testimony by telling the jury that Satterwhite was beyond the reach of psychiatric rehabilitation. The prosecutor noted Dr. Grigson's credentials and conclusions in his closing argument.

> [Doctor James Grigson, a Dallas psychiatrist and medical doctor] tells you that on a range from 1 to 10 he's ten plus. Severe sociopath. Extremely dangerous. A continuing threat to our society. Can it be cured? Well it's not a disease. It's not an illness. That's his personality. That's John T. Satterwhite.

This concluding statement must have influenced the jury. Certainly, it was meant to. The High Court reversed the judgment of the Texas Court of Criminal Appeals insofar as it upheld the death penalty.

Needing a Psychiatrist to Prove Insanity

Late in 1979, Glen Burton Ake allegedly murdered a couple and wounded their two children. He was arrested and arraigned in Canadian County, Oklahoma. His behavior, both at the arraignment and while being held, was so bizarre that the trial judge ordered Ake examined by a psychiatrist to determine if he should be put under a lengthy period of mental observation. The examining psychiatrist reported "at times [Ake] appears to be frankly delusional.... He claims to be the 'sword of vengeance' of the Lord and that he will sit at the left hand of God in heaven." The psychiatrist diagnosed the defendant as a probable paranoid schizophrenic and recommended a prolonged psychiatric evaluation to determine whether he was competent to stand trial.

Consequently, Ake was committed to a state hospital on the basis of his "present sanity," and the chief forensic psychiatrist at the state hospital informed the court Ake was not competent to stand trial. Furthermore, during the competency hearing, the psychiatrist concluded,

> [Ake] is a psychotic ... his psy-
> chiatric diagnosis was that of
> paranoid schizophrenia — chronic,
> with exacerbation, that is with
> current upset, and that in addition ...
> he is dangerous ... [B]ecause of the
> severity of his mental illness and
> because of the intensities of his rage,
> his poor control, his delusions, he
> requires a maximum security facility
> within — I believe — the State
> Psychiatric Hospital system."

Based on this testimony, the court found Ake to be a "mentally ill person in need of care and treatment" and incompetent to stand trial, and ordered him committed to the state mental hospital.

Six weeks later, the chief forensic psychiatrist informed the court that Ake had become competent to stand trial. Ake was receiving 200 milligrams of Thorazine, a drug used to calm difficult psychiatric patients, three times a day, and the psychiatrist indicated that if Ake continued to receive this daily dose, he would remain stable for a trial. The State of Oklahoma resumed proceedings against the accused murderer.

At a pre-trial conference, Ake's lawyer told the court his client would raise a defense of insanity. Therefore, in order to adequately defend himself, Ake would have to be examined by a psychiatrist to determine his mental condition at the time of the crime. While at the state hospital, no doctor had tried to determine Ake's sanity at the time of the crime, and, as an indigent (a poor person), he could not afford to pay for a psychiatrist. Ake's counsel asked the court to provide a psychiatrist or the money to allow the defense to hire one. The trial judge refused his request.

During the trial, Ake's sole defense was insanity. The defense counsel called to the stand the psychiatrists who had examined Ake at the state hospital, but none had determined his sanity at the time of the crime. The prosecution, in turn, asked the doctors if they could speak on the accused's mental state at the time of the crime, and each doctor replied that he could not. *As a result, there was no expert testimony for either side on Ake's sanity at the time of the offense.* (Italics are from the release of the Supreme Court. See below.) The judge then instructed the jurors that Ake could be found not guilty by reason of insanity if he did not have the ability to distinguish right from wrong at the time of the alleged offense. They were further told that Ake was to be presumed sane at the time of the crime unless *he* (italics from the release of the Supreme Court) presented evidence sufficient to raise a reasonable doubt about his sanity at that time. The jury rejected Ake's insanity defense and returned a verdict of guilty on all counts.

During the sentencing phase of the trial, the prosecution relied upon the earlier testimony of the state psychiatrists who had examined Ake and found that, at this time, the defendant was dangerous to society. Ake had no expert witness to rebut this testimony or to introduce evidence on his behalf in mitigation of his punishment. The jury sentenced Ake to death.

The Oklahoma Court of Criminal Appeals saw no reason why the state was obligated to pay for a psychiatrist for poor defendants and upheld the conviction. An 8-1 U.S. Supreme Court, in *Ake v. Oklahoma* (470 US 68, 1985), did and reversed the lower court's ruling. The High Court observed that

> This Court has long recognized that when a State brings its judicial power to bear on an indigent defendant in a criminal proceeding, it must take steps to assure that the defendant has a fair opportunity to present his defense. This elementary principle, grounded in significant part on the Fourteenth Amendment's due process guarantee of fundamental fairness, derives from the belief that justice cannot be equal where, simply as a result of his poverty, a defendant is denied the opportunity to participate meaningfully in a judicial proceeding in which his liberty is at stake....

> We recognized long ago that mere access to the courthouse doors does not by itself assure a proper functioning of the adversary process, and that a criminal trial is fundamentally unfair if the State proceeds against an indigent defendant without making certain that he has access to the raw materials integral to the building of an effective defense.

The justices felt the State of Oklahoma had a direct interest in the fair and accurate findings of the jury. Consequently, the claim that providing a psychiatrist would impose "a staggering burden" on the state carried no weight. While "neither approv[ing] nor disapprov[ing] the widespread reliance on psychiatrists," the Court recognized their increasing importance and necessity over the last 40 years in determining sanity and other states of mental condition. Noting that it had been left to juries to resolve the disagreements among psychiatrists, the justices believed that a defendant without a psychiatrist is left at a serious disadvantage.

> Without the assistance of a psychiatrist to conduct a professional examination on issues relevant to the defense, to help determine whether the insanity defense is viable, to present testimony, and to assist in preparing the cross-examination of a State's psychiatric witnesses, the risk of an inaccurate resolution of sanity issues is extremely high.

This overall finding would also apply during the sentencing phase when the jury is asked to consider the future danger to society represented by the accused. Therefore, the Supreme Court concluded that Ake was entitled to the assistance of a psychiatrist, reversed the lower court rulings, and sent the case back for a new trial.

CAN AN INSANE PERSON BE EXECUTED?

Alvin Ford was convicted of murder in 1974 and sentenced to death. There is no question that he was completely sane at the time of his crime, the trial, and the sentencing. In early 1982, however, Ford began to show peculiar signs of delusion. He eventually believed that the Ku Klux Klan, the prison guards, and many others were conspiring to force him to commit suicide. He believed the guards were killing people and that his female relatives were being tortured and raped somewhere in the prison. He believed 135 of his friends and family were being held hostage in the prison and that he was Pope John Paul II.

Ford's lawyer requested a psychiatrist to examine his client, and after 14 months of study, the doctor found Ford suffered from "a severe, uncontrollable, mental disease which closely resembles 'Paranoid Schizophrenia With Suicide Potential'" —a "major mental disorder ... severe enough to substantially affect Mr. Ford's present ability to assist in the defense of his life." Ford later refused to see the psychiatrist and was interviewed by a second psychiatrist who concluded, "Ford had no understanding of why he was being executed, made no connection between the homicide of which he had been convicted and the death penalty, and indeed sincerely believed that he would not be executed because he owned the prisons and could control the Governor through mind waves." The second doctor thought Ford was definitely not faking his insanity.

Florida law required the governor to appoint a panel of three psychiatrists to determine whether Ford had "the mental capacity to understand the nature of the death penalty and the reasons why it was imposed upon him." At a single meeting, the three doctors interviewed Ford for approximately 30 minutes and then filed separate reports. While Ford's lawyers were present, the governor ordered specifically that "the attorneys should not participate in the examination in any adversarial manner." While the three psychiatrists reached somewhat different conclusions, they all agreed that Ford was sane enough to be executed. Ford's lawyers attempted to submit the reports of the first two psychiatrists who had studied Ford, along with other materials, but the governor would not indicate whether he would consider them. Without comment, the governor signed Ford's death warrant.

Ford's appeals were denied in state and federal courts, but a 7-2 Supreme Court, in *Ford v. Wainwright* (477 US 399, 1986), reversed the earlier judgments. "For centuries no jurisdiction has countenanced the execution of the insane, yet this Court has never decided whether the Constitution forbids the practice. Today we keep faith with our common-law heritage in holding that it does." Writing for the majority, Justice Marshall observed that, while the reasons appear unclear, English Common Law forbade the execution of the insane. The English jurist Blackstone had labeled such a practice "savage and inhuman," while the other noted English judicial resource, Sir Edward Coke, believed such executions "of extreme inhumanity and cruelty, and can be no example to others." The Court knew "of virtually no authority condoning the execution of the insane at English common law." Consequently, since the Eighth Amendment, forbidding "cruel and unusual punishment" was prepared by men who accepted English common law, there could be no question that the Eighth Amendment prohibited the execution of the insane.

The issue then became the method of determining Ford's insanity in the state of Florida. Forbidding Ford's lawyers to question the psychiatrists denied the defense the opportunity to bring

> to light the bases for each expert's beliefs, the precise factors underlying those beliefs, any history of error or caprice of the examiner, any personal bias with respect to the issue of capital punishment, the expert's degree of certainty about his or her own conclusions, and the precise meaning of ambiguous words used in their report.

"Perhaps the most striking defect in the procedures," said the Court, was the placement of the decision wholly within the executive branch. The governor's subordinates had been responsible for prosecuting Ford. Now the governor would appoint the psychiatrists and then make the final decision. "The commander of the State's corps of prosecutors cannot be said to have the neutrality that is necessary for reliability in the fact finding proceeding." Finally, as noted in Justice O'Connor's partially concurring opinion, "if there is one 'fundamental requisite' of due process, it is that an individual is entitled to an 'opportunity to be heard.' " The Florida law did not require that the governor consider materials submitted by the prisoner, and the "present Governor has a 'publicly announced policy of excluding' such materials from his consideration." Such a law and policy, stated Justice O'Connor, invited "arbitrariness and error" and was not "fair." The majority seemed to think a trial might be necessary to determine sanity, while Justice O'Connor thought that "a constitutionally acceptable procedure may be far less formal than a trial," perhaps an impartial officer or a board.

In dissent, Justice Rehnquist, joined by Chief Justice Burger, thought the Florida procedure consistent with English Common Law, which had left the decision to the executive and further worried that

> A claim of insanity may be made at any time before sentence and, once rejected, may be raised again; a prisoner found sane two days before execution might claim to have lost his sanity the next day, thus necessitating another judicial determination of his sanity and presumably another stay of his execution.

CAN A MENTALLY RETARDED PERSON BE EXECUTED?

Pamela Carpenter was brutally raped, beaten, and stabbed with a pair of scissors. Before she died, she was able to describe her attacker, and as a result, Johnny Penry was arrested for, and later confessed to, the crime. He was found guilty and sentenced to die. Among the issues considered in his appeal was whether the State of Texas could execute a mentally retarded person. Johnny Penry had been tested over the years as having an IQ between 50 and 63, which indicates mild to moderate retardation. The court testimony and appeals generally agreed that Penry had the mental age of a 6 ½ year child and the social maturity of a 9- to 10-year-old. The Supreme Court generally accepted these findings. During his childhood, he had been abused.

Concerning the issue of mental retardation, Penry's attorneys argued that

because of their mental disabilities, mentally retarded people do not possess the level of moral culpability to justify imposing the death sentence.... there is an emerging national consensus against executing the retarded.

Writing for the five-person majority (Justices O'Connor, Rehnquist, White, Scalia, and Kennedy) on the question of executing a mentally-retarded person, Justice O'Connor, in *Penry v. Lynaugh* (492 US 302, 1989), found no emerging national consensus against the execution of mentally retarded defendants. Furthermore, while historically idiots and profoundly retarded persons have not been executed for murder, Penry did not fall into this group.

Justice O'Connor noted that Penry was found competent to stand trial — "In other words, he was found to have the ability to consult with his lawyer with a reasonable degree of rational understanding, and was found to have a rational as well as factual understanding of the proceedings against him."

Justice O'Connor thought that the defense was guilty of lumping all mentally retarded together, as if no differences distinguished them. "I cannot conclude," the Justice observed,

> that all mentally retarded people of Penry's ability — by virtue of their mental retardation alone, and apart from any individualized consideration of their personal responsibility — inevitably lack the cognitive, volitional, and moral capacity to act with the degree of culpability associated with the death penalty. Mentally retarded persons are individuals whose abilities and experiences can vary greatly.

If the mentally retarded were not treated as individuals, but as an undifferentiated group, a mildly mentally retarded person could be denied the opportunity to enter into contracts or to marry by virtue of the fact that he had a "mental age" of a young child. In light of the diverse capacities and life experiences of mentally retarded persons, it cannot be said on the record before us today that all mentally retarded people, by definition, can never act with the level of culpability associated with the death penalty.

Justice O'Connor also believed the concept of "mental age" likely underestimated the value of the life experiences of the mentally retarded person while overvaluing the ability to use logic and foresight to solve problems.

Finally, the majority could find no national movement toward any type of consensus on this issue. While *Penry* produced several public opinion polls that indicated strong public opposition to executing the retarded, almost none of this public opinion was reflected in death-penalty legislation. Only the federal Anti-Drug Abuse Act of 1988 (PL 100-690) and the State of Georgia banned the execution of retarded persons who have been found guilty of a capital crime. Certainly, concluded Justice O'Connor, a single federal law and a single state statute did "not provide sufficient evidence at present of a national consensus."

Justice Brennan disagreed.

> [F]or many purposes, legal and otherwise, to treat the mentally retarded as a homogeneous group is inappropriate, bringing the risk of false stereotyping and unwarranted discrimination. Nevertheless, there are characteristics as to which there is no danger of spurious generalization because they are a part of the clinical definition of mental retardation.

Citing the *amicus* brief prepared by the American Association on Mental Retardation, Justice Brennan noted that

> Every individual who has mental retardation — irrespective of her precise capacities or experiences — has a substantial disability in cognitive ability and adaptive behavior.... Though individuals, particularly those who are mildly retarded, may be quite capable of overcoming these limitations to the extent of being able to maintain themselves independently or semi-independently in the community, nevertheless, the mentally retarded by definition have a reduced ability to cope with and function in the everyday world.

Since the mentally retarded are, by definition, less than fully responsible for their actions, just as children are, they should not face the death penalty. Finally, Justice Brennan did not believe that executing a person not fully responsible for his or her actions would further the penal goals of either retribution or deterrence. What is the point of executing someone who did not fully recognize the terrible evil which he or she had done? Furthermore, executing a mentally retarded person would not deter non-retarded people, those who would be aware of an execution, since they are already subject to being executed.

COMPETENCY STANDARD

The Supreme Court, in *Godinez v. Moran* (113 S.Ct. 2708, 1993), considered whether the competency standard for pleading guilty or waiving the right to counsel is higher than the competency standard for standing trial.

The petitioner was sentenced to death by a Nevada jury for fatally shooting a bartender and patron four times each and his former wife five times with an automatic pistol. Two psychiatrists examined the defendant and concluded that he was competent to stand trial. Approximately 10 weeks after the evaluations, the defendant decided to discharge his attorneys and change his pleas to guilty. After review of the defendant's mental condition, the trial court accepted the waiver for counsel and the guilty pleas. The defendant was then sentenced to death. He appealed to the Court of Appeals for the Ninth Circuit claiming that he had been mentally incompetent to represent himself. The Court of Appeals reversed the conviction, ruling that the conviction was based upon a legal standard for competency that was too low.

In a 7-to-2 decision, the Supreme Court reversed the judgment of the Court of Appeals, holding that the decision to waive the right to counsel does not require a higher level of mental functioning than the decision to waive other constitutional rights. The Court held that the standard for measuring a criminal defendant's competency to plead guilty or to waive the right to counsel is not higher than the standard for standing trial.

RACE AS A CONSIDERATION

On July 12, 1978, Willie Turner, a Black man, robbed a jewelry store in Franklin, Virginia. Angered because the owner had set off a silent alarm, Turner first shot the owner in the head, wounding him, and then shot him twice in the chest, killing him for "snitching." Included among the questions submitted for consideration by Turner's lawyer was

> The defendant, Willie Lloyd Turner, is a member of the Negro race. The victim, W. Jack Smith, Jr., was a white Caucasian. Will these facts prejudice you against Willie Lloyd Turner or affect your ability to render a fair and impartial verdict based solely on the evidence?

The judge refused to allow this question to be asked. A jury of 8 Whites and 4 Blacks convicted Turner and then, in a separate sentencing hearing, recommended the death sentence, which the judge imposed.

Turner appealed his conviction, claiming that the judge's refusal to ask prospective jurors about their racial attitudes deprived him of his right to a fair trial. Although his argument failed to convince state and federal appeals courts, the U.S. Supreme Court chose to hear his case, and in *Turner v. Murray* (476 US 28, 1986), the High Court, in a 7-2 decision, overturned Turner's death sentence (but not the conviction).

Writing for the majority, Justice White noted that in considering a death sentence, the jury is called upon to make a "highly subjective, unique, individualized judgment regarding the punishment, that a particular person deserves." Judge White further observed that

> Because of the range of discretion entrusted to a jury in a capital sentencing hearing, there is a unique opportunity for racial prejudice to operate but remain undetected. On the facts of this case, a juror who believes that blacks are violence-prone or morally inferior might well be influenced by that belief in deciding whether petitioner's crime involved the aggravating factors specified under Virginia law. Such a juror might also be less favorably inclined toward petitioner's evidence of mental disturbance as a mitigating circumstance. More subtle, less consciously held racial attitudes could also influence a juror's decision in this case. Fear of blacks, which could easily be stirred up by the violent facts of petitioner's crime, might incline a juror to favor the death penalty.

The Court has recognized that "the qualitative difference of death from all other punishments requires a correspondingly greater degree of scrutiny of the capital sentencing determination." The judge, by not asking prospective jurors about their racial attitudes, had not exercised this "greater degree of scrutiny," and the Supreme Court reversed the death sentence against Turner.

The High Court, however, did not reverse Turner's conviction and Justice Brennan, who agreed with the reversal of the sentence, wondered why the concern for racial biases "should be of less concern at the guilt phase than at the sentencing phase." "Might not that same juror," Justice Brennan asked, "be influenced by those same prejudices in deciding whether, for example, to credit or discredit white witnesses as opposed to black witnesses at the guilt phase? Might not these same racial fears that would incline a juror to favor death not also incline a juror to favor conviction?" Justice Brennan felt the Court expressed proper concern that a defendant not be sentenced to death by a prejudiced jury, but then was inconsistent when it seemed not to be similarly concerned that the defendant be convicted by the same jury.

Justice Powell, in his dissent, thought that the High Court had recognized "a presumption that jurors who have sworn to decide the case impartially nevertheless are racially biased." Furthermore, Justice Powell felt that this meant that any case involving a Black and a White would have to consider the racial issue and that this did not necessarily follow.

Limits to Consideration
of Racial Attitudes

Warren McCleskey and three other armed men robbed a furniture store in Fulton County, Georgia. A police officer, responding to a silent alarm, entered the store, was shot twice, and died. McCleskey was Black; the officer he was convicted of murdering was White. McCleskey admitted taking part in the robbery, but denied shooting the policeman. The state proved that at least one shot came from the weapon McCleskey was carrying and produced two witnesses who had heard McCleskey admit to the shooting. A jury found him guilty and McCleskey, offering no mitigating circumstances during the sentencing phase, was sentenced to death.

McCleskey eventually appealed his case all the way to the U.S. Supreme Court. Part of his appeal was based upon two major statistical studies of 2,000 Georgia murder cases that occurred during the 1970s prepared by Professors David Baldus, George Woodworth, and Charles Pulanski (referred to as the Baldus Study). The Baldus Study found that defendants charged with killing White persons received the death penalty in 11 percent of cases, but defendants charged with killing Blacks received the death penalty in only 1 percent of the cases. Furthermore, the death penalty was given in 22 percent of the cases involving Black defendants and White victims, 8 percent of the cases involving White defendants and White victims, 1 percent of the cases involving Black defendants and Black victims, and 3 percent of the cases involving White defendants and Black victims.

Similarly, the Baldus study found that prosecutors sought the death penalty in 70 percent of the cases involving Black defendants and White victims; 32 percent of the cases involving White defendants and White victims; 15 percent of the cases involving Black defendants and Black victims; and 19 percent of the cases involving White defendants and Black victims. Finally, after taking account of variables that could have explained the differences on nonracial grounds, the study concluded that defendants charged with killing White victims were 4.3 times as likely to receive a death sentence as defendants charged with killing Blacks.

Dr. Baldus further argued that the effects of racial bias were most striking in the mid-range cases. In courtroom testimony, Baldus stated that "when the cases become tremendously aggravated [really brutal cases] so that everybody would agree that if we're going to have a death sentence, these are the cases that should get [the death sentence], the race effects go away. It's only in the mid-range cases where the decision-makers have a real choice as to what to do. If there's room for the exercise of discretion, then the [racial] factors begin to play a role." (Dr. Baldus considered McCleskey's case a mid-range murder.) While the federal district court did not accept the Baldus study, both the U.S. Court of Appeals and the U.S. Supreme Court accepted the study as valid.

The District Court and the Court of Appeals rejected McCleskey's appeal and, in *McCleskey v. Kemp* (481 US 279, 1987), so did a 5-4 split U.S. Supreme Court. McCleskey had to show that the State of Georgia had acted in a discriminatory manner in his case and the Baldus study was "clearly insufficient to support an inference that any of the decision makers in McCleskey's case acted with discriminatory purpose." "Statistics," observed Judge Powell for the majority, "at most may show only a likelihood that a particular factor entered into some decisions. There is, of course, some risk of racial prejudice influencing a jury's decision," but the majority believed previous rulings had built in enough safeguards to guarantee equal protection for every defendant. "At most," declared the Court,

> the Baldus study indicates a discrepancy that appears to correlate with race. Apparent disparities in sentencing are an inevitable part of our criminal justice system.... any mode for determining guilt or punishment "has its weaknesses and the potential for misuse." "There can be no perfect procedure for deciding in which cases governmental authority should be used to impose death."... Where the discretion that is fundamental to our criminal process is involved, we decline to assume that what is unexplained is invidious.... We hold that the Baldus study [while we do not argue with its findings] does not demonstrate a constitutionally significant risk of racial bias.

The Court expressed concern that if they found that Baldus's findings did represent a risk, it might well be applied to lesser cases. It further noted that it is the job of the legislative branch to consider these findings and incorporate them into the laws to guarantee equal protection in courts of law.

Justice Brennan, who, along with Justice Marshall, believed capital punishment "is in all circumstances cruel and unusual punishment" and therefore unconstitutional, thought that the findings of the Baldus study powerfully showed "the intractable reality of the death penalty; that the effort to eliminate arbitrariness in the infliction of that ultimate sanction is so plainly doomed to failure that it — and the death penalty — must be abandoned altogether." As a result, the Court cannot rely on the "statutory safeguards" to guarantee a Black defendant a fair sentencing. While the Baldus Study did not show that racism necessarily led to McCleskey's death sentence, it had surely shown that McCleskey faced a considerably greater likelihood of being sentenced to death because he was a Black man convicted of killing a White man.

Also writing in dissent, Justice Blackmun thought the majority had concentrated too much on the potential racial attitudes of the jury. As important, he thought were the racial attitudes of the prosecutor's office, which the Baldus Study found to be much more likely to seek the death penalty for a Black who had killed a White than other categories. The district attorney for Fulton County had testified that no county policy existed on how capital cases were prosecuted and that death penalty "decisions were left to the discretion of the individual attorneys who then informed [the district attorney] of their decisions as they saw fit." Certainly such a system was open to abuse. Without guidelines, the racial prejudices of the prosecuting attorneys could play a significant role in deciding whether or not to seek the death penalty. Prosecutors, indeed, needed significant leeway in making their decisions, but they were not "beyond the constraints imposed on state action under the Fourteenth Amendment" guaranteeing fair due process. Nor could Georgia's history of racial prejudice be totally dismissed as past history, as the Court majority had done. While it should not be the overriding factor, it certainly was no longer "irrelevant" and should certainly be considered in any case presented to the High Court. Justice Blackmun concluded that the High Court's concern that, if the Baldus findings were upheld, they might be applied to other cases was no grounds to rule as they had.

If a grant of relief to McCleskey were to lead to a closer examination of the effects of racial considerations throughout the criminal justice system, the system, and society, might benefit. Where no such factors come into play, the integrity of the system is enhanced. Where racial considerations are shown to be significant, efforts can be made to eliminate their impermissible influence and to ensure an evenhanded application of criminal sanctions.

Justice Stevens, in his dissent, agreed, noting that affirming the Baldus study would not mean an end to the death penalty, but, rather, "the danger of arbitrary and discriminatory imposition of the death penalty would be significantly decreased, if not eradicated."

The Race of Jurors and Equal Protection

A grand jury in Coweta County, Georgia, indicted James A. Ford, a Black man, for the kidnaping, rape, and murder of a White woman. The state informed Ford that it planned to seek the death penalty. Before the trial, Ford filed a "Motion to Restrict Racial Use of Peremptory Challenges," alleging that Coweta County had "over a long period of time" excluded Black persons from juries "where the issues to be tried involved members of the opposite race." The motion indicated that Ford "anticipated" that the pattern of racial exclusion would continue in this case because the accused was Black and the victim was White.

At a pretrial hearing, Ford's lawyer noted that it had been his experience that the district attorney and others in his office had used their peremptory challenges (the right not to chose a juror without giving a reason) to excuse potential Black jurors. Ford's lawyer asked the trial judge to prevent this by ordering the district attorney to justify on the record his reasons for excusing potential Black jurors. If the prosecutor failed to offer justification, it would show that he was "using his peremptory challenges in a discriminatory manner." The prosecution denied that there was proof of discrimination. He referred to the U.S. Supreme Court decision in *Swain v. Alabama* (380 U.S. 202, 1965) which said, in part, "it would be an unreasonable burden to require an attorney for either side to justify his use of peremptory [sic] challenges." The judge responded that he had seen several cases of the district attorney's passing over prospective White jurors in favor of potential Black jurors and because of that observation was denying the motion to restrict racial use of peremptory challenges.

The prosecution used nine of its 10 peremptory challenges to strike prospective Black jurors, leaving only one Black member seated on the jury. This Black member was challenged by Ford's attorney, not by the district attorney. In closed sessions, Ford's attorney observed for the record that nine of the 10 Black prospective members had been dismissed on peremptory challenges by the district attorney. The judge agreed and allowed the observation for the record, but told the prosecutor that he did not have to offer any reasons for his peremptory actions. Ford was convicted on all counts and was sentenced to death. His attorney called for a new trial and claimed that Ford's "right to an impartial jury as guaranteed by Sixth Amendment [calling for a fair cross-section of the community] to the United States Constitution was violated by the prosecutor's exercise of his peremptory challenges on a racial basis."

The Supreme Court of Georgia affirmed the conviction, stating that Ford had failed to prove the "systematic exclusion of Black jurors" from the jury and found no error. Ford appealed to the U.S. Supreme Court, which had ruled in *Batson v. Kentucky* (476 US 79, 1986), which dropped the *Swain* requirement of proof of prior discrimination, that a Black criminal could make a *prima facie* case of an equal protection violation with evidence that the prosecutor had used peremptory challenges in his case to strike members of the defendant's race from the jury. Reversing the decision of the Georgia Supreme Court, the U.S. Supreme Court vacated Ford's conviction and ruled that *Batson*'s new standard could be applied retroactively (*Ford v. Georgia*, 59 LW 411, 1991).

Delivering the opinion for a unanimous Court, Justice Souter held that the Georgia Supreme Court had erred when it ruled that Ford had failed to present a proper equal protection claim, "although he certainly failed to do it with the clarity that appropriate citations would have promoted." Although Ford's pretrial motion did not mention the Equal Protection Clause, and his new trial motion had cited the Sixth Amendment rather than the Fourteenth, the motion referring to a pattern of excluding Black members "over a long period of time asserts an equal protection claim."

METHODS OF EXECUTION

Lethal Injection May Be Used for Executions

The injection of a deadly combination of drugs has become the method of execution in most states permitting capital punishment. Condemned prisoners from Texas and Oklahoma, two of the first states to introduce this method, brought suit claiming that while the drugs used had been approved by the Food and Drug Administration (FDA) for medical purposes, they had never been approved for use in nor tested for human executions. Furthermore, since the drugs would likely be administered by untrained personnel, they might not cause the quick and painless death intended. The petitioners alleged that these drugs had been "misbranded," a violation of 21 U.S.C. para. 352 (f), which states "A drug or device shall deemed to be misbranded ... [u]nless its labeling bears (1) adequate directions for use...." In addition, since the drugs were being put to a new use, they had to be reapproved by the FDA to determine if they were "safe and effective" for human execution.

The FDA Commissioner refused to act, claiming serious questions as to whether the agency had jurisdiction in the area. He further noted that

> Generally, enforcement proceedings in this area are initiated only when there is a serious danger to the public health or a blatant scheme to defraud. We cannot conclude that those dangers are present under State lethal injections laws, which are duly authorized statutory enactments in furtherance of proper State [goals].

The condemned prisoners disagreed, claiming that the FDA did indeed have a responsibility to determine if the lethal mixture injected during execution was "safe and effective." The United States District Court for the District of Columbia disagreed, noting that decisions by a federal agency not to take action were not reviewable in court. A divided Court of Appeals for the District of Columbia reversed the lower District Court ruling, noting the FDA's own policy required the FDA to investigate the unapproved use of an approved drug when such use became "widespread" or "endanger[ed] the public health." Therefore, the prisoners, who risked a "cruel and protracted" death were entitled to a more thorough investigation of the drugs used in their execution.

A generally irritated Supreme Court agreed to hear the case "to review the implausible result that the FDA is required to exercise its enforcement power to ensure that States use only drugs that are 'safe and effective' for human execution." In *Heckler v. Chaney* (470 US 821, 1985), the unanimous Court agreed that, in this case, the FDA did not have jurisdiction, although Justices Brennan and Marshall indicated that the limitation on court jurisdiction should not apply to all agency decisions not to intervene, while the remaining justices thought the courts had no right to question any agency decision not to take action.

Writing for all but Justices Marshall and Brennan, Justice Rehnquist explained why the majority of justices concluded the FDA decision not to investigate the prisoner's request was simply not the High Court's business.

First, an agency decision not to enforce often involves a complicated balancing of a number of factors which are peculiarly within its expertise. Thus, the agency must not only assess where a violation has occurred, but whether agency resources are best spent on this violation or another, whether the agency is likely to succeed if it acts, whether the particular enforcement action requested best fits the agency's overall policies, and indeed, whether the agency has enough resources to undertake the action at all. An agency generally cannot act against each technical violation of the statute it is charged with enforcing. The agency is better equipped than the courts to deal with the many variables involved in the proper ordering of its priorities.

Based on these observations, the majority of the Court concluded that "an agency's decision not to take enforcement action should be presumed immune from judicial review." Only a decision by Congress requesting judicial intervention could justify a judicial role in monitoring agency actions. While agreeing with the majority in this case, Justices Brennan and Marshall felt that while "deference" should be given to an agency's decision not to review, this did not mean immunity from judicial review applied in all instances.

Are Executions by Hanging and Gas Chambers Constitutional?

Hanging

A Washington State law provides for capital punishment either by "hanging by the neck" or, at the choice of the condemned, by lethal injection.

In *Campbell v. Wood* (CA 9, (en banc), No. 89-35210, 1994), the Ninth Court of Appeals found that "execution, as administered in Washington, is not cruel and unusual punishment forbidden by the Eighth Amendment." Decisions concerning the Eighth Amendment focus on whether the sentence constitutes "one of the 'modes or acts of punishment that had been considered cruel and unusual at the time that the Bill of Rights was adopted' " and on whether the punishment is contrary to "the evolving standards of decency that mark the progress of a maturing society" (*Trop v. Dulles*, 356 US 86, 1958).

Of course, when the Bill of Rights was adopted, hanging was an acceptable punishment. However, the second question on contemporary standards is more difficult to answer. The courts usually assume that a punishment chosen by a democratically elected legislature is constitutionally valid. However, the respondent, Campbell, who had been convicted of first-degree murder in Washington, argued that only two states (Washington and Montana) used hanging as a method of execution. He relied on *Coker v. Georgia* and *Edmund v. Florida* (see Chapter II) for the idea that "when the number of states exacting a given punishment dwindles, the punishment drops beneath the constitutional floor." However, those cases dealt with the types of crimes to which the death penalty applied, not the method of execution.

The court continued that it could not decide whether hanging violates the Eighth Amendment by counting the number of states using it as a method of execution. Hanging cannot be considered cruel and unusual because it causes death or

because there may be some pain associated with death. As used in the constitution, "cruel" implies "something inhuman and barbarous, something more than the mere extinguishment of life." *In re Kemmler*, 136 U.S. 436 (1890). Campbell is entitled to an execution free only of "the unnecessary and wanton infliction of pain." *Gregg*.

The court continued that the "mechanisms involved in bringing about unconsciousness and death in judicial hanging occur extremely rapidly" and that "risk of death by decapitation was negligible," and that "hanging, according to the method used by the state, did not involve lingering death, mutilation or the unnecessary and wanton infliction of pain." Thus the Washington law allowing hanging did not violate the Eighth Amendment. The case was appealed, and the Supreme Court denied *certiori* (114 S.Ct. 2125), letting the lower court ruling stand.

Gas Chambers

On October 4, 1994, a federal district judge in California, Marilyn Hall Patel, ruled that execution by lethal gas "is inhumane and has no place in civilized society" and ordered California's gas chamber closed and that lethal injection be used. This was the first time a federal judge ruled that any method of execution violated the Eighth Amendment. While the State of California maintained that cyanide gas caused almost instant unconsciousness, the judge referred to doctors' reports and witnesses' accounts of gas chamber executions that indicated that the dying inmates stayed conscious for 15 seconds to a minute or longer and suffered "intense physical pain." California's Attorney General said that he would appeal the ruling. No executions were scheduled at that time, but lethal injection could be used, as it was an option the legislature had passed in 1993.

FUTURE CONSIDERATIONS

While the recent history of capital punishment shows a reluctance to impose the ultimate penalty and is marked by confusion and sometimes even contradiction, the grounds for appeal are becoming narrower. Many observers believe that the time is drawing near when all constitutional issues will have been raised and decided and the condemned will have no more recourse to the courts to postpone an execution. The federal judges have also made it harder for inmates to continually petition the federal courts by establishing limits on *habeas corpus* reviews. Then inmates' lives will be in the hands of the state governors and, as a general rule, governors have not commuted death sentences.

CHAPTER V

DEATH PENALTY STATUTES AND METHODS

CAPITAL OFFENSES

Most death penalty statutes (laws) in force prior to the *Furman v. Georgia* decision of June 29, 1972, provided for the imposition of the death penalty for capital murder and, in some states, for other crimes. (See Chapter II.) However, in *Furman*, the United States Supreme Court found that the death penalty, as then being administered, was "cruel and unusual punishment" in violation of the Eighth Amendment of the U.S. Constitution. Many states revised their laws to conform to standards set by the *Furman* decision and, subsequently, by other decisions that determined the validity of revised statutes. Since *Furman*, review of individual state statutes has continued as appeals of capital sentences reach state courts or the U.S. Supreme Court.

Under revised state laws, different types of capital murder have been specifically defined. Although varying somewhat from one jurisdiction to another, the types of homicide most commonly specified are murder carried out during the commission of another felony; murder of a peace officer, corrections employee, or fireman engaged in the performance of official duties; murder by an inmate serving a life sentence; and murder for hire (contract murder). Different statutory terminology may be used by different states to designate basically identical crimes; in some states, such terms as "murder," "first-degree murder," "murder Class A felony," etc., may indicate the same capital offense.

While there are other offenses (most notably, treason and air piracy or hijacking) which carry the death penalty, most have not yet had their constitutionality tested. The Supreme Court has held, in *Everheart v. Georgia* and *Coker v. Georgia* (433 US 584, 1977), that rape and kidnaping which do not result in death do not warrant the death penalty. (See Chapter IV.) Nonetheless, Mississippi still permits the death penalty for the forcible rape of a child under 14 years old by a person 18 years or older. A new Louisiana law allows for the death penalty in rape cases if the victim is less than 12 years old. At year-end 1994, the death penalty was authorized by the statutes of 38 states and by federal legislation. Table 5.1 lists the capital offenses for various states.

RECENT STATUTORY CHANGES

Twelve states during 1993 and 14 states during 1994 revised statutory provisions relating to the death penalty. Nearly all of the changes defined circumstances for which capital punishment may be applied, additional categories of victims permitting the application of the death penalty, and broadening of the law to allow a defendant to choose between two methods of execution.

1993

Among changes made in 1993, Arizona provided that persons sentenced to death shall not be executed if they are mentally ill or incompetent and cannot understand the nature of the punishment or the reasons for the execution. Colorado also revised its statute to prohibit the execution of mentally retarded persons. Arkansas

TABLE 5.1

**Capital offenses, by State,
Alabama through Maryland, 1994**

Alabama. Murder during kidnaping, robbery, rape, sodomy, burglary, sexual assault, or arson; murder of a peace officer, correctional officer, or public official; murder while under a life sentence; murder for pecuniary gain or contract; aircraft piracy; murder by a defendant with a previous murder conviction; murder of a witness to a crime; murder when a victim is subpoenaed in a criminal proceeding, when the murder is related to the role of the victim as a witness; murder when a victim is less than 14 years old; murder in which a victim is killed while in a dwelling by a deadly weapon fired or otherwise used from outside the dwelling; murder in which a victim is killed while in a motor vehicle by a deadly weapon; murder in which a victim is killed by a deadly weapon fired or otherwise used in or from a motor vehicle (13A-5-40).

Arizona. First-degree murder accompanied by at least 1 of 10 aggravating factors.

Arkansas. Capital murder as defined by Arkansas statute (5-10-101). Felony murder; arson causing death; intentional murder of a law enforcement officer, teacher or school employee; murder of prison, jail, court, or correctional personnel or of military personnel acting in line of duty; multiple murders; intentional murder of a public officeholder or candidate; intentional murder while under life sentence; contract murder.

California. Treason; homicide by a prisoner serving a life term; first-degree murder with special circumstances; train wrecking; perjury causing execution.

Colorado. First-degree murder; felony murder; intentionally killing a peace officer, firefighter, judge, referee, elected State, county, or municipal official, Federal law enforcement officer or agent; person kidnaped or being held hostage by the defendant or an associate of the defendant; being party to an agreement to kill another person; murder committed while lying in wait, from ambush, or by use of an explosive or incendiary device; murder for pecuniary gain; murder in an especially heinous, cruel, or depraved manner; murder for the purpose of avoiding or preventing a lawful arrest or prosecution or effecting an escape from custody , including the intentional killing of a witness to a criminal offense; killing 2 or more persons during the same incident and murder of a child less than 12 years old; treason. Capital sentencing excludes persons determined to be mentally retarded.

Connecticut. Murder of a public safety or correctional officer; murder for pecuniary gain; murder in the course of a felony; murder by a defendant with a previous conviction for intentional murder; murder while under a life sentence; murder during a kidnaping; illegal sale of cocaine, methadone, or heroin to a person who dies from using these drugs; murder during first-degree sexual assault; multiple murders; the defendant committed the offense(s) with an assault weapon.

Delaware. First-degree murder with aggravating circumstances, including murder of a child victim 14 years of age or younger by an individual who was at least 4 years older than the victim; killing of a nongovernmental informant who provides an investigative, law enforcement or police agency with information concerning criminal activity; and premeditated murder resulting from substantial planning.

Federal prison system.

Florida. Felony murder; first-degree murder; sexual battery on a child under age 12; destructive devices (unlawful use resulting in death). Capital drug trafficking.

Georgia. Murder; kidnaping with bodily injury when the victim dies; aircraft hijacking; treason; kidnaping for ransom when the victim dies.

Idaho. First-degree murder; aggravated kidnaping.

Illinois. First-degree murder accompanied by at least 1 of 14 aggravating factors.

Indiana. Murder with 14 aggravating circumstances.

Kansas. Capital murder, including intentional and premeditated killing of any person in the commission of kidnaping; contract murder; intentional and premeditated killing by a jail or prison inmate; intentional and premeditated killing in the commission of rape or sodomy; intentional and premeditated killing of a law enforcement officer; and intentional and premeditated killing of a child under the age of 14 in the commission of kidnaping. Killing 2 or more persons during the same incident.

Kentucky. Murder with aggravating factor; kidnaping with aggravating factor.

Louisiana. First-degree murder; treason (La. R.S. 14:30 and 14:113).

Maryland. First-degree murder, either premeditated or during the commission of a felony, provided that certain death eligibility requirements are satisfied.

(Continued)

added teachers and other school employees to its capital-murder victims list that includes law enforcement officers, prison officials, probation and parole officers, firefighters, and court officials, while Illinois added paramedics, ambulance drivers, and other medical assistance personnel to its list. Texas added to its list of capital offenses the murder of more than one person during the same criminal transaction; murder of more than one person during different criminal transactions, but according to the same scheme or course of conduct; and murder of an individual under age 6.

TABLE 5.1 (Continued)

Mississippi through Wyoming

Mississippi. Capital murder includes murder of a peace officer or correctional officer, murder while under a life sentence, murder by bomb or explosive, contract murder, murder committed during specific felonies (rape, burglary, kidnaping, arson, robbery, sexual battery, unnatural intercourse with a child, nonconsensual unnatural intercourse), and murder of an elected official. Capital rape is the forcible rape of a child under 14 years old by a person 18 years or older. Aircraft piracy.

Missouri. First-degree murder (565.020 RSMO).

Montana. Deliberate homicide; aggravated kidnaping when victim or rescuer dies; attempted deliberate kidnaping by a State prison inmate who has a prior conviction for deliberate homicide or who has been previously declared a persistent felony offender (46-18-303,MCA).

Nebraska. First-degree murder.

Nevada. First-degree murder with 9 aggravating circumstances.

New Hampshire. Capital murder, including contract murder; murder of a law enforcement officer; murder of a kidnaping victim; killing another after being sentenced to life imprisonment without parole.

New Jersey. Purposeful or knowing murder; contract murder.

New Mexico. First-degree murder; felony murder with aggravating circumstances.

North Carolina. First-degree murder (N.C.G.S. 14-17).

Ohio. Aggravated murder, including assassination; contract murder; murder during escape; murder while in a correctional facility; murder after conviction for a prior purposeful killing or prior attempted murder; murder of a peace officer; murder arising from specified felonies (rape, kidnaping, arson, robbery, burglary); murder of a witness to prevent testimony in a criminal proceeding or in retaliation (O.R.C. secs. 2929.02, 2903.01, 2929.04).

Oklahoma. First-degree murder, including murder with malice aforethought; murder arising from specified felonies (forcible rape, robbery with a dangerous weapon, kidnaping, escape from lawful custody, first-degree burglary, arson); murder when the victim is a child who has been injured, tortured, or maimed.

Oregon. Aggravated murder.

Pennsylvania. First-degree murder.

South Carolina. Murder with a statutory aggravating circumstance.

South Dakota. First-degree murder; kidnaping with gross permanent physical injury inflicted on the victim; felony murder.

Tennessee. First-degree murder.

Texas. Murder of a public safety officer, fireman, or correctional employee; murder during the commission of specified felonies (kidnaping, burglary, robbery, aggravated rape, arson); murder for remuneration; multiple murders; murder during prison escape; murder of a correctional officer; murder by a State prison inmate who is serving a life sentence for any of five offenses; murder of an individual under 6 years of age.

Utah. Aggravated murder. Aggravated assault by a prisoner serving a life sentence if serious bodily injury is intentionally caused (76-5-202, Utah Code annotated).

Virginia. Murder during the commission or attempts to commit specified felonies (abduction, armed robbery, rape, forcible sodomy); contract murder; murder by a prisoner while in custody; murder of a law enforcement officer; multiple murders; murder of a child under 12 years during an abduction; murder arising from drug violations (18.2-31, Virginia Code as amended).

Washington. Aggravated first-degree premeditated murder.

Wyoming. Premeditated murder; felony murder in the perpetration (or attempts) of sexual assault, arson, robbery, burglary escape, resisting arrest, kidnaping, or abuse of a child under 16 years of age.

Source: *Capital Punishment 1994*, Bureau of Justice Statistics, Washington, DC, 1996

1994

Among the changes made in 1994, Colorado added to its capital-punishment statute the murder of two or more persons during the same criminal episode and the intentional killing of a child under age 12. Delaware included the murder of a child age 14 or younger by a person at least 4 years older than the victim, the killing of a nongovernmental informant in retaliation for providing information concerning criminal activity, and premeditated murder resulting from "substantial planning." New Jersey also added the murder of a person younger than 14 years of age, while Tennessee changed its law to cover victims younger than 16. Maryland's new law states that anyone sentenced to death shall be executed by lethal injection. Persons sentenced to death by lethal gas prior to March 25, 1994, will be executed by lethal injection unless a written request was made within 60 days after March 25, 1994. The federal Violent Crime Control and Law Enforcement Act of 1994 (PL 103-322) expanded the federal death penalty to cover more than 50 offenses.

MINIMUM AGE FOR EXECUTION

The United States has executed an estimated 285 juvenile offenders. The first execution of a juvenile occurred in 1642 in Plymouth Colony (located in modern day Massachusetts) for the crime of bestiality (having sexual intercourse with an animal). The youngest person to be executed in this century was George J. Stinney Jr., a Black youth of 14 years, in South Carolina in 1944.

By 1995, only eight jurisdictions did not specify a minimum age for which the death penalty may be imposed. Thirteen states and the federal death penalty require a minimum age of 18; 16 states indicate various ages of eligibility between 14 and 17 (Table 5.2). In some states the minimum age is determined by state laws that define the age at which a juvenile may be

TABLE 5.2

Minimum age authorized for capital punishment, 1994

Age less than 18	Age 18	None specified
Alabama (16)	California	Arizona
Arkansas (14)[a]	Colorado	Idaho
Delaware (16)	Connecticut[d]	Montana
Georgia (17)	Federal system	Louisiana
Indiana (16)	Illinois	Pennsylvania
Kentucky (16)	Kansas	South Carolina
Mississippi (16)[b]	Maryland	South Dakota[e]
Missouri (16)	Nebraska	Utah
Nevada (16)	New Jersey	
New Hampshire (17)	New Mexico	
North Carolina (17)[c]	Ohio	
Oklahoma (16)	Oregon	
Texas (17)	Tennessee	
Virginia (15)	Washington	
Wyoming (16)		
Florida (16)		

Note: Reporting by States reflects interpretations by State attorney general offices and may differ from previously reported ages.

[a]See Arkansas Code Ann.9-27-318(b)(1)(Repl. 1991).

[b]Minimum age defined by status is 13, but effective age is 16 based on an interpretation of U.S. Supreme Court decisions by the State attorney general's office.

[c]Age required is 17 unless the murderer was incarcerated for murder when a subsequent murder occurred; the age then may be 14.

[d]See Conn. Gen. Stat. 53a-46a(g)(1).

[e]Juveniles may be transferred to adult court. Age may be a mitigating circumstance. No one under age 10 can commit a crime.

Source: *Capital Punishment 1994*, Bureau of Justice Statistics, Washington, DC, 1996

transferred to the criminal court for trial as an adult. Once a minor is tried as an adult, he or she may then face the same penalties (including death) to which an adult may be sentenced. The Supreme Court has held that a minor as young as 16 years old may be executed. (See Chapter IV.)

EXECUTING MENTALLY RETARDED PERSONS

In 1988, Georgia became the first state to prohibit the execution of murderers found "guilty, but mentally retarded." The legislation resulted from the 1986 execution of Jerome Bowden, who had an I.Q. of 65 (normal I.Q. is considered 90 and above), and from Georgia Supreme Court rulings suggesting the Georgia state legislature reconsider the situation.

In 1990, Missouri and Tennessee also passed legislation limiting the sentencing of mentally retarded individuals convicted of murder to life imprisonment, not death. In 1992, South Carolina allowed mental retardation to be used as a mitigating circumstance in deciding punishment for murder. As stated above, in 1993, Arizona revised its statutes to prevent the execution of the mentally ill or incompetent, and Colorado prohibited the execution of mentally retarded persons.

The federal government, in the Anti-Drug Law of 1988 (PL 100-690), permits the death penalty for any person working "in furtherance of a continuing criminal enterprise or any person engaging in a drug-related felony offense, who intentionally kills or counsels, commands, or causes the intentional killing of an individual," but forbids the imposition of the death penalty against anyone who is mentally retarded who commits this particular crime.

FEDERAL DEATH PENALTY LAWS

The federal laws providing for the death penalty are listed below.

8 U.S.C. 1342 — Murder related to the smuggling of aliens.

10 U.S.C. 906(a) — Espionage by a member of the Armed Forces: communication of information to a foreign government relating to nuclear weaponry, military spacecraft or satellites, early warning systems, war plans, communications intelligence or cryptographic information, or any other major weapons or defense strategy.

10 U.S.C. 918 — Murder while a member of the Armed Forces.

18 U.S.C. 32-34 — Destruction of aircraft, motor vehicles, or related facilities resulting in death.

18 U.S.C. 36 — Murder committed during a drug-related drive-by shooting.

18 U.S.C. 37 — Murder committed at an airport serving international civil aviation.

18 U.S.C. 115(b)(3) [by cross-reference to 18 U.S.C. 1111] — Retaliatory murder of a member of the immediate family of law enforcement officials.

18 U.S.C. 241, 242, 245, 247 — Civil rights offenses resulting in death.

18 U.S.C. 351 [by cross-reference to 18 U.S.C. 1111] — Murder of a member of Congress, an important executive official, or a Supreme Court Justice.

18 U.S.C. 794 — Espionage.

18 U.S.C. 844(d),(f), (I) — Death resulting from offenses involving transportation of explosives, destruction of government property or the destruction of property related to foreign or interstate commerce.

18 U.S.C. 924 (1) — Murder committed by the use of a firearm during a crime of violence or a drug-trafficking crime.

18 U.S.C. 930 — Murder committed in a federal government facility.

18 U.S.C. 1091 — Genocide.

18 U.S.C. 1111 — First-degree murder.

18 U.S.C. 1114 — Murder of a federal judge or law enforcement official.

18 U.S.C. 1116 — Murder of a foreign official.

18 U.S.C. 1118 — Murder by a federal prisoner.

18 U.S.C. 1119 — Murder of a U.S. national in a foreign country.

18 U.S.C. 1120 — Murder by an escaped federal prisoner already sentenced to life imprisonment.

18 U.S.C. 1121 — Murder of a state or local law enforcement officer or other person aiding in a federal investigation; murder of a state correctional officer.

18 U.S.C. 1203 — Murder during a hostage-taking.

18 U.S.C. 1503 — Murder of a court officer or juror.

18 U.S.C. 1512 — Murder with the intent of preventing testimony by a witness, victim, or informant.

18 U.S.C. 1513 — Retaliatory murder of a witness, victim, or informant.

18 U.S.C. 1716 — Mailing of injurious articles with intent to kill or resulting in death.

18 U.S.C. 1751 [by cross-reference to 18 U.S.C. 1111] — Assassination or kidnaping resulting in the death of the president or vice president.

18 U.S.C. 1958 — Murder for hire.

18 U.S.C. 1959 — Murder involved in a racketeering offense.

18 U.S.C. 1992 — Willful wrecking of a train resulting in death.

18 U.S.C. 2113 — Bank-robbery-related murder or kidnaping.

18 U.S.C. 2119 — Murder related to carjacking.

18 U.S.C. 2245 — Murder related to rape or child molestation.

18 U.S.C. 2251 — Murder related to sexual exploitation of children.

18 U.S.C. 2280 — Murder committed during an offense against maritime navigation.

18 U.S.C. 2281 — Murder committed during an offense against a maritime fixed platform.

18 U.S.C. 2332 — Terrorist murder of a U.S. national in another country.

18 U.S.C. 2332a — Murder by the use of a weapon of mass destruction.

18 U.S.C. 2340 — Murder involving torture.

18 U.S.C. 2381 — Treason.

21 U.S.C. 841(b)(A) or section 9960(b)(1); and 21 U.S.C. 848(e) — (A) any person engaging in or working in furtherance of a continuing criminal enterprise, or any person engaging in an offense punishable under section 960(b)(1) who intentionally kills or counsels, commands, induces, procures, or causes the intentional killing of an individual and such killing results, shall be sentenced to any term of imprisonment, which shall not be less than 20 years, and which may be up to life imprisonment, or may be sentenced to death; and (B) any person, during the commission of, in furtherance of, or while attempting to avoid apprehension, prosecution, or service of a prison sentence for a felony violation of this subchapter or subchapter II of this chapter who intentionally kills or counsels, commands, induces, procures, or causes the intentional killing of any Federal, State, or local law enforcement officer engaged in, or on account of, the performance of such officer's official duties and such killing results, shall be sentenced to any term of imprisonment, which shall not be less than 20 years, and which may be up to life imprisonment, or may be sentenced to death (21 U.S.C. para 848(e)).

DEATH PENALTY METHODS

The Eighth Amendment of the United States Bill of Rights continues the prohibition of "cruel and unusual punishment" called for in the English Bill of Rights of 1689. While the Salem witchcraft trials witnessed a single case of pressing to death (placing an individual between two hard surfaces and applying pressure until the person is dead) and some rebellious Blacks were burned at the stake during the first part of the eighteenth century, these were exceptional cases.

For the most part, neither the colonies nor the United States ever suffered excesses such as drawing and quartering, burying alive, boiling in oil, sawing in half, or crucifixion. Throughout most of the nineteenth century, hanging was the prescribed method of civilian execution, while the military preferred to shoot spies, traitors, and deserters.

Currently, only Delaware, Montana, New Hampshire, and Washington use the gallows, while use of the firing squad is restricted to Utah. In January 1996, Delaware hanged a condemned prisoner. It was the state's first hanging in 50 years and the nation's third execution by hanging since 1965. Washington hanged two murderers in 1993 and 1994. Also, in January 1996, Utah executed its first prisoner by firing squad since 1977 when Gary Gilmore was executed. (See Chapter II.)

The five states that execute by either hanging or shooting offer the condemned the alternative of lethal injection. A total of 14 states authorize more than one method — lethal injection and an alternative method — generally letting the condemned prisoner choose. However, five of these 14 states specify which method must be used, depending on the date of sentencing. New Hampshire authorized hanging only if lethal injection could not be given, and Wyoming authorized lethal gas if lethal injection is ever held to be unconstitutional. (See Table 5.3.)

Electrocution

At the end of the nineteenth century, alternating current electricity became one of the dominant symbols of progress. It followed that many people thought this modern convenience would provide an apparently more humane method of execution so, in 1893, the first without warning, while sleeping. A practical method of carrying out that specified method could not be arranged so a gas chamber was constructed. In 1924, cyanide gas was used for the first time to execute a condemned man. In 1994, seven states used lethal gas. In 1994, a federal judge in California ruled that lethal gas was an inhumane method (see Chapter IV). (See Table 5.3.)

Lethal Injection

Over the past several years, most states practicing capital punishment have adopted the injection of a lethal drug as a more humanitarian alternative to other methods. Following several legal challenges, the Supreme Court, in *Heckler v. Chaney* (53 LW 4385, 1984), upheld the use of lethal drug injection. (See Chapter IV.) As of 1994, 27 states and the federal system now use injection, either solely or as an alternative to another method. (See Table 5.3.)

TABLE 5.3

Method of execution, by State, 1994

Lethal Injection	Electrocution	Lethal gas	Hanging	Firing squad
Arizona[a,b]	Alabama	Arizona[a]	Delaware[a,c]	Utah[a]
Arkansas[a,d]	Arkansas[a,d]	California[a]	Montana[a]	
California[a]	Connecticut	Maryland[a,e]	New Hampshire[a,f]	
Colorado	Florida	Mississippi[a,g]	Washington[a]	
Delaware[a,c]	Georgia	Missouri[a]		
Idaho	Indiana	North Carolina[a]		
Illinois	Kentucky	Wyoming[a,h]		
Kansas	Nebraska			
Louisiana	Ohio[a]			
Maryland[a,e]	South Carolina			
Mississippi[a,g]	Tennessee			
Missouri[a]	Virginia			
Montana[a]				
Nevada				
New Hampshire[a,f]				
New Jersey				
New Mexico				
North Carolina[a]				
Ohio[a]				
Oklahoma				
Oregon				
Pennsylvania				
South Dakota				
Texas				
Utah[a]				
Washington[a]				
Wyoming[a]				

Note: The method of execution of Federal prisoners is lethal injection, pursuant to 28 CFR, Part 26. For offenses under the Violent Crime Control and Law Enforcement Act of 1994, the method is that of the State in which the conviction took place, pursuant to 18 USC 3596.

[a] Authorizes 2 methods of execution.

[b] Arizona authorizes lethal injection for persons whose capital sentence was received after 11/15/92; for those sentenced before that date, the condemned may select lethal injection or lethal gas.

[c] Delaware authorizes lethal injection for those whose capital offense occurred after 6/13/86; for those whose offense occurred before that date, the condemned may select lethal injection or hanging.

[d] Arkansas authorizes lethal injection for those whose capital offense occurred after 7/4/83; for those whose offense occurred before that date, the condemned may select lethal injection or electrocution.

[e] Maryland authorizes lethal injection for those whose capital offense occurred after 3/25/94 and also for those whose offense occurred before that date, unless within 60 days from that date, the condemned selected lethal gas.

[f] New Hampshire authorizes hanging only if lethal injection cannot be given.

[g] Mississippi authorizes lethal injection for those convicted after 7/14/84 and lethal gas for those convicted prior to that date.

[h] Wyoming authorizes lethal gas if lethal injection is ever held to be unconstitutional.

Source: *Capital Punishment 1994*, Bureau of Justice Statistics, Washington, DC, 1996

condemned man was put to death in a crude electric chair. Currently, 12 states use electrocution. (See Table 5.3.)

Lethal Gas

In 1921, the Nevada legislature authorized the use of lethal gas. The actual bill called for the condemned person to be executed in his cell,

PUBLIC AND PRIVATE EXECUTIONS

Early arguments for capital punishment centered around the issue of deterrence. Therefore, executions were held in public in an attempt to inhibit anyone from contemplating the same deed as the condemned. Many of these executions were held in a circus atmosphere, causing some to oppose such a public display. In 1830, the State of New York recommended that executions take place in private, but it still remained the decision of the local sheriff. Five years later, the state legislature prohibited public executions.

The idea caught on slowly and, even where executions were confined to jail courtyards, it was often not difficult to find a perch from which to watch the hanging. By the end of the century, private executions had become standard, although many public executions still took place. The last public hanging was in 1936, in Owensboro, Kentucky, where a Black man was hanged before 20,000 spectators. The holiday atmosphere, recorded on wire service photographs, caused such a reaction that the Kentucky legislature banned public executions two years later.

Today all states limit the number of witnesses, although in celebrated cases, such as the Rosenbergs, convicted spies (1953), and Caryl Chessman, a notorious California killer (1960), the audience, swelled by reporters, grew to several dozen. The idea of private executions was introduced to appease abolitionists, but today some opponents of capital punishment support the idea of returning to public executions. They feel that private executions hide the act from the public and make it more acceptable, and some have even recommended televised executions. On the other hand, some proponents of the death penalty support public executions hoping that they might act as a deterrent to future murderers.

Victim's Family as Witnesses

Virginia, California, Louisiana, Delaware, and Texas allow victims' families to view the execution. In Delaware, the two sons of the victim watched the hanging of their father's murderer in January 1996. In February 1996, family members of the victim witnessed an execution in Texas. These family members believed that they could finally be able to put closure to their tragedy.

Videotape

In 1994, a videotape of the execution of Robert Alton Harris (1992) was ordered destroyed by court order. The tape was made to be used in a federal lawsuit challenging the constitutionality of the gas chamber. (See Chapter IV.) The tape was not used in the trial because the state did not challenge the accounts of witnesses to Mr. Harris's execution. William Bennet Turner, a lawyer who represented the television station KQED which had brought suit unsuccessfully to have cameras in the execution chamber, commented, "It's the only videotape of an American execution ever. I don't understand the reason for its destruction."

CHAPTER VI

HISTORICAL STATISTICS*

HOW MANY EXECUTIONS?

From 1930, when national reporting began, through 1994, there were 4,116 executions conducted under civil authority in the United States (Figure 6.1 and Tables 6.1 and 6.2). Table 6.1 shows the number of executions by jurisdiction and time period, breaking down the statistics for five-year periods through 1979. (Table 6.1, taken from the *Sourcebook of Criminal Justice Statistics* and based on the Bureau of Justice (BJS) data, does not include the 31 executions carried out in 1994.) Table 6.2 also shows the number of executions by jurisdiction, but it ranks the jurisdictions by total number of prisoners executed from 1930 to 1994.

The number of executions generally declined between the 1930s and the 1960s, and in 1967, a

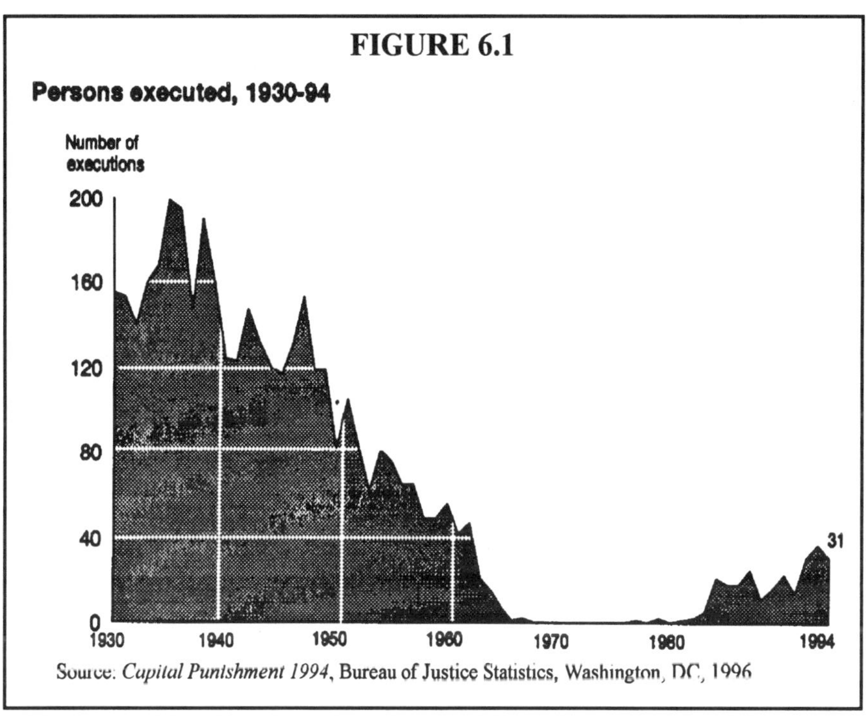

Source: *Capital Punishment 1994*, Bureau of Justice Statistics, Washington, DC, 1996

10-year moratorium began, as states waited for the Supreme Court to determine a constitutionally acceptable procedure for carrying out the death penalty. (See Chapter II.) The first execution after the moratorium ended took place in Utah in 1977. Since then, according to the Bureau of Justice Statistics, U.S. Department of Justice, as of

---

*The statistics and charts used throughout this chapter and the next were prepared by the United States Department of Justice, Bureau of Justice Statistics, which collects and distributes such information. Additional information was supplied by the NAACP Legal Defense and Educational Fund, Inc. (LDF) of New York, a nationally recognized, private organization which collects information on capital punishment. The LDF is no longer a part of the National Association of Colored People (NAACP), although it was founded by that organization and shares its commitment to equal rights and opposition to capital punishment. THE LDF has had a separate board of directors, program, staff, office, and budget for over 30 years. The LDF publishes a quarterly, "Death Row, USA," which counts the total number of death-row inmates, the number executed since January 1, 1973, and other information on capital punishment in America.

Prisoners executed under civil authority

By region and jurisdiction, 1930-93

(- represents zero)

Region and jurisdiction	Total	1930 to 1934	1935 to 1939	1940 to 1944	1945 to 1949	1950 to 1954	1955 to 1959	1960 to 1964	1965 to 1969	1970 to 1974	1975 to 1979	1980 to 1982	1983	1984	1985	1986	1987	1988	1989	1990	1991	1992	1993
United States	4,085	776	891	645	639	413	304	181	10	-	3	3	5	21	18	18	25	11	16	23	14	31	38
Federal	33	1	9	7	6	6	3	1	-	-	-	-	-	-	-	-	-	-	-	-	-	-	-
State	4,052	775	882	638	633	407	301	180	10	-	3	3	5	21	18	18	25	11	16	23	14	31	38
Northeast	608	155	145	110	74	56	51	17	-	-	-	-	-	-	-	-	-	-	-	-	-	-	-
Connecticut	21	2	3	5	5	-	5	1	-	-	-	-	-	-	-	-	-	-	-	-	-	-	-
Maine	X	X	X	X	X	X	X	X	X	X	X	X	X	X	X	X	X	X	X	X	X	X	X
Massachusetts	27	7	11	6	3	-	-	-	-	-	-	X	-	X	X	X	X	X	X	X	X	X	X
New Hampshire	1	-	1	-	-	-	-	-	-	-	-	-	-	-	-	-	-	-	-	-	-	-	-
New Jersey	74	24	16	6	8	8	9	3	-	-	X	-	-	-	-	-	-	-	-	-	-	-	-
New York	329	80	73	78	36	27	25	10	-	-	-	-	-	X	X	X	X	X	X	X	X	X	X
Pennsylvania	152	41	41	15	21	19	12	3	-	-	-	-	-	-	-	-	-	-	-	-	-	-	-
Rhode Island	-	-	-	-	-	-	-	-	-	-	-	X	X	X	X	X	X	X	X	X	X	X	X
Vermont	4	1	-	-	1	2	-	-	-	-	-	-	-	-	-	-	-	-	-	-	X	X	X
Midwest	417	105	113	42	64	42	16	16	5	-	-	1	-	-	1	-	-	-	1	5	1	1	4
Illinois	91	34	27	13	5	8	1	2	-	-	-	-	-	-	-	-	-	-	-	1	-	-	-
Indiana	43	11	20	2	5	2	-	1	-	-	-	1	-	-	1	-	-	-	-	-	-	-	-
Iowa	18	1	7	3	4	1	-	2	X	X	X	X	X	X	X	X	X	X	X	X	X	X	X
Kansas	15	X	-	3	2	5	-	1	4	-	X	X	X	X	X	X	X	X	X	X	X	X	X
Michigan	-	-	-	-	-	-	-	-	X	X	X	X	X	X	X	X	X	X	X	X	X	X	X
Minnesota	X	X	X	X	X	X	X	X	X	X	X	X	X	X	X	X	X	X	X	X	X	X	X
Missouri	73	16	20	6	9	5	2	3	1	-	-	-	-	-	-	-	-	-	1	4	1	1	4
Nebraska	4	-	-	-	2	1	1	-	-	-	-	-	-	-	-	-	-	-	-	-	-	-	-
North Dakota	-	-	-	-	-	-	-	-	-	-	-	X	X	X	X	X	X	X	X	X	X	X	X
Ohio	172	43	39	15	36	20	12	7	-	-	-	-	-	-	-	-	-	-	-	-	-	-	-
South Dakota	1	X	-	-	1	-	-	-	-	-	-	-	-	-	-	-	-	-	-	-	-	-	-
Wisconsin	X	X	X	X	X	X	X	X	X	X	X	X	X	X	X	X	X	X	X	X	X	X	X
South	2,502	419	524	413	419	244	183	102	2	-	1	2	5	21	16	18	24	10	13	17	13	26	30
Alabama	145	19	41	29	21	14	6	4	1	-	-	-	1	-	-	1	1	-	4	1	-	2	-
Arkansas	122	20	33	20	18	11	7	9	-	-	-	-	-	-	-	-	-	-	-	2	-	2	-
Delaware	15	2	6	2	2	-	-	-	-	-	-	-	-	-	-	-	-	-	-	-	-	1	2
District of Columbia	40	15	5	3	13	3	1	-	-	-	X	X	X	X	X	X	X	X	X	X	X	X	X
Florida	202	15	29	38	27	22	27	12	-	-	1	-	1	8	3	3	1	2	2	4	2	2	3
Georgia	383	64	73	58	72	51	34	14	-	-	-	-	1	2	3	1	5	1	1	-	1	-	2
Kentucky	103	18	34	19	15	8	8	1	-	-	-	-	-	-	-	-	-	-	-	-	-	-	-
Louisiana	154	39	19	24	23	14	13	1	-	-	-	-	1	5	1	-	8	3	-	1	1	-	1
Maryland	68	6	10	26	19	2	4	1	-	-	-	-	-	-	-	-	-	-	-	-	-	-	-
Mississippi	158	26	22	34	26	15	21	10	-	-	-	-	1	-	-	-	2	-	1	-	-	-	-
North Carolina	268	51	80	50	62	14	5	1	-	-	-	-	-	2	-	1	-	-	-	-	1	1	-
Oklahoma	63	25	9	6	7	4	3	5	1	-	-	-	-	-	-	-	-	-	-	1	-	2	-
South Carolina	166	37	30	32	29	16	10	8	-	-	-	-	-	-	1	1	-	-	-	1	1	-	-
Tennessee	93	16	31	19	18	1	7	1	-	-	-	-	-	-	-	-	-	-	-	-	-	-	-
Texas	368	48	72	38	36	49	25	29	-	-	-	1	-	3	6	10	6	3	4	4	5	12	17
Virginia	114	8	20	13	22	15	8	6	-	-	-	1	-	1	2	1	1	1	1	3	2	4	5
West Virginia	40	10	10	2	9	5	4	-	X	X	X	X	X	X	X	X	X	X	X	X	X	X	X
West	525	96	100	73	76	65	51	45	3	-	2	-	-	-	1	-	1	1	2	1	-	4	4
Alaska[a]	X	X	X	X	X	X	X	X	X	X	X	X	X	X	X	X	X	X	X	X	X	X	X
Arizona	41	7	10	8	3	2	6	4	-	-	-	-	-	-	-	-	-	-	-	-	-	1	2
California	294	51	57	35	45	39	35	29	1	-	-	-	-	-	-	-	-	-	-	-	-	1	1
Colorado	47	16	9	6	7	1	2	5	1	-	-	-	-	-	-	-	-	-	-	-	-	-	-
Hawaii[a]	X	X	X	X	X	X	X	X	X	X	X	X	X	X	X	X	X	X	X	X	X	X	X
Idaho	3	-	-	-	-	2	1	-	-	-	-	-	-	-	-	-	-	-	-	-	-	-	-
Montana	6	1	4	1	-	-	-	-	-	-	-	-	-	-	-	-	-	-	-	-	-	-	-
Nevada	34	5	3	5	5	9	-	2	-	-	1	-	-	-	1	-	-	-	2	1	-	-	-
New Mexico	8	2	-	-	2	2	1	1	-	-	-	-	-	-	-	-	-	-	-	-	-	-	-
Oregon	19	1	1	6	6	4	-	1	X	X	-	-	X	-	-	-	-	-	-	-	-	-	-
Utah	17	-	2	3	1	2	4	1	-	-	1	-	-	-	-	-	1	1	-	-	-	1	-
Washington	48	10	13	9	7	4	2	2	-	-	-	-	-	-	-	-	-	-	-	-	-	-	1
Wyoming	8	3	1	2	-	-	-	-	-	-	-	-	-	-	-	-	-	-	-	-	-	1	-

Note: In three States, Maine, Minnesota, and Wisconsin, there was no death penalty for the entire period covered by the table. Alaska and Hawaii have not had the death penalty since 1960, when they were first included as States. For other States, the death penalty may have been abolished or declared unconstitutional, and/or subsequently reinstated. In these cases, an X will appear to indicate years when the death penalty was not in effect.

[a] As States, Alaska and Hawaii are included in the series beginning Jan. 1, 1960.

Source: U.S. Department of Justice, Bureau of Justice Statistics, *Correctional Populations in the United States, 1993*, NCJ-156241 (Washington, DC: U.S. Department of Justice, 1995), Table 7.25. Table adapted by SOURCEBOOK staff.

Source: Kathleen Maguire and Ann L. Pastore, eds., *Sourcebook of Criminal Justice Statistics — 1994*, U.S. Department of Justice, Bureau of Justice Statistics, Washington, DC; USGPO, 1995

TABLE 6.2

Number of persons executed, by jurisdiction, 1930-94

State	Number executed Since 1930	Since 1977
U.S. total	4,116	257
Georgia	384	18
Texas	382	85
New York	329	
California	294	2
North Carolina	269	6
Florida	203	33
Ohio	172	
South Carolina	166	4
Mississippi	158	4
Louisiana	154	21
Pennsylvania	152	
Alabama	145	10
Arkansas	127	9
Virginia	116	24
Kentucky	103	
Tennessee	93	
Illinois	92	2
New Jersey	74	
Missouri	73	11
Maryland	69	1
Oklahoma	63	3
Washington	49	2
Colorado	47	
Indiana	44	3
Arizona	41	3
District of Columbia	40	
West Virginia	40	
Nevada	34	5
Federal system	33	
Massachusetts	27	
Connecticut	21	
Oregon	19	
Iowa	18	
Utah	17	4
Delaware	16	4
Kansas	15	
New Mexico	8	
Wyoming	8	1
Montana	6	
Nebraska	5	1
Idaho	4	1
Vermont	4	
New Hampshire	1	
South Dakota	1	
Alaska	0	
Hawaii	0	
Maine	0	
Michigan	0	
Minnesota	0	
North Dakota	0	
Rhode Island	0	
Wisconsin	0	

Source: *Capital Punishment 1994*,
Bureau of Justice Statistics,
Washington, DC, 1996

TABLE 6.3

PRISONERS EXECUTED UNDER CIVIL AUTHORITY
IN THE UNITED STATES,
BY YEAR AND STATES

YEAR	TOTAL	STATE
1990	23	FL(4), MO(4), TX(4),VA(3), AR(2), AL(1), IL(1), OK(1), LA(1), NV(1), SC(1)
1991	14	TX(4), FL(2), VA(2), LA(1), MO(1), NC(1), SC(1), Un known(2)
1992	31	TX(13), VA(3), FL(2), AL(2), AR(2), OK(2), NC(1), MO(1), UT(1), WY(1), CA(1), AZ(1), DE(1)
1993	34	TX(14), VA(5), MO(4), FL(3), DE(2), AZ(2) CA(1), GA(1), LA(1), WA(1)
1994	31	TX (14), AR (5), VA (2), DE (1), FL (1), GE (1), ID,(1), IL (1), IN (1), MD (1), NE (1), NC (1), WA (1)
1995*	45	TX (15), VA (4), IL (4) OK (3), MO (3), GA (2), AR (2), AL (2), PA (2), NC (2) MT (1), DE (1), AZ (1), LA (1), FL (1), SC (1)

*as of 10/31/95

Source: Updated by staff of Information Plus from "Death Row USA," Fall 1995, prepared by the NAACP Legal Defense and Education Fund, Inc.

December 31, 1994, 257 executions took place. According to the NAACP Legal Defense Fund, a non-profit organization that collects information on capital punishment, 302 persons were executed in the United States from 1977 to October 31, 1995.

WHERE ARE THE EXECUTIONS?

Over the past half century, approximately 3 out of every 5 executions took place in the South. Of the 257 executions since 1977, all but 35 were in the South. Since 1930, the largest single number (384), more than 9 percent of the total, occurred in Georgia. Forty percent of all executions were carried out in just five states: Georgia, Texas, New York, California, and North Carolina. Between 1977 and 1994, 24 states executed prisoners, led by Texas with 85; Florida with 33; Virginia, 24; Louisiana, 21; and Georgia, 18. These states accounted for 70 percent of all executions during this period. (See Tables 6.2 and 6.3.)

In 1994, Texas again had the greatest number of executions (14). Arkansas put 5 inmates to death and Virginia executed 2 prisoners. Delaware, Florida, Georgia, Idaho, Illinois, Indiana, Maryland, Nebraska, North Carolina, and Washington each had one execution. From January 1, 1995, through October 31, 1995, Texas executed 15 prisoners. Virginia and Illinois put 4 inmates to death. Oklahoma and Missouri had 3 executions each; Georgia, Arkansas, Alabama, Pennsylvania, and North Carolina each executed 2 inmates. Six other states each had one execution. (See Table 6.3.)

GENDER

Between 1930 and 1993, 33 women were put to death (Table 6.4). The NAACP Legal Defense Fund statistics from 1977 through October 1995 show only one woman was executed; thus, while Table 6.4 shows only information through 1990, it is current.

TABLE 6.4

Female prisoners executed under civil authority

By offense, race, and jurisdiction, United States, 1930-90

(- represents zero)

Year	Total	Offense		Race		Jurisdiction in which executed
		Murder	Other[a]	White	Black	
1930-90	33	31	2	21	12	X
1984	1	1	-	1	-	North Carolina
1962	1	1	-	1	-	California
1957	1	1	-	1	-	Alabama
1955	1	1	-	1	-	California
1954	2	2	-	1	1	Ohio
1953	3	1	2	3	-	Alabama, Federal (Missouri and New York)
1951	1	1	-	1	-	New York
1947	2	2	-	1	1	California, South Carolina
1946	1	1	-	-	1	Pennsylvania
1945	1	1	-	-	1	Georgia
1944	3	3	-	-	3	Mississippi, New York, North Carolina
1943	3	3	-	1	2	Mississippi, North Carolina, South Carolina
1942	1	1	-	1	-	Louisiana
1941	1	1	-	1	-	California
1938	2	2	-	2	-	Illinois, Ohio
1937	1	1	-	-	1	Mississippi
1936	1	1	-	1	-	New York
1935	3	3	-	2	1	Delaware, Louisiana, New York
1934	1	1	-	1	-	New York
1931	1	1	-	1	-	Pennsylvania
1930	2	2	-	1	1	Arizona, Alabama

No females were executed in the years that are not listed.

[a]Includes one kidnaping and one espionage case (both Federal).

Source: U.S. Department of Justice, Bureau of Justice Statistics. *Capital Punishment 1984*, NCJ-99562, Table 4; *1986*, Bulletin NCJ-106483. p. 9, Appendix table 2; *1988*, Bulletin NCJ-118313, p. 2; *1989*. Bulletin NCJ-124545, p. 2 (Washington, DC: U.S. Department of Justice). Table adapted by SOURCEBOOK staff.

TABLE 6.5

Prisoners executed under civil authority

By race and offense, United States, 1930-93

(- represents zero)

	Total				White				Black				Other			
	Total	Murder	Rape	Other offenses[a]	Total	Murder	Rape	Other offenses	Total	Murder	Rape	Other offenses	Total	Murder	Rape	Other offenses
1930-93	4,085	3,560	455	70	1,887	1,800	48	39	2,154	1,718	405	31	44	42	2	-
1993	38	38	-	-	23	23	-	-	14	14	-	-	1	1	-	-
1992	31	31	-	-	19	19	-	-	11	11	-	-	1	1	-	-
1991	14	14	-	-	7	7	-	-	7	7	-	-	-	-	-	-
1990	23	23	-	-	16	16	-	-	7	7	-	-	-	-	-	-
1989	16	16	-	-	8	8	-	-	8	8	-	-	-	-	-	-
1988	11	11	-	-	6	6	-	-	5	5	-	-	-	-	-	-
1987	25	25	-	-	13	13	-	-	12	12	-	-	-	-	-	-
1986	18	18	-	-	11	11	-	-	7	7	-	-	-	-	-	-
1985	18	18	-	-	11	11	-	-	7	7	-	-	-	-	-	-
1984	21	21	-	-	13	13	-	-	8	8	-	-	-	-	-	-
1983	5	5	-	-	4	4	-	-	1	1	-	-	-	-	-	-
1982	2	2	-	-	1	1	-	-	1	1	-	-	-	-	-	-
1981	1	1	-	-	1	1	-	-	-	-	-	-	-	-	-	-
1980	-	-	-	-	-	-	-	-	-	-	-	-	-	-	-	-
1979	2	2	-	-	2	2	-	-	-	-	-	-	-	-	-	-
1978	-	-	-	-	-	-	-	-	-	-	-	-	-	-	-	-
1977[b]	1	1	-	-	1	1	-	-	-	-	-	-	-	-	-	-
1967	2	2	-	-	1	1	-	-	1	1	-	-	-	-	-	-
1966	1	1	-	-	1	1	-	-	-	-	-	-	-	-	-	-
1965	7	7	-	-	6	6	-	-	1	1	-	-	-	-	-	-
1964	15	9	6	-	8	5	3	-	7	4	3	-	-	-	-	-
1963	21	18	2	1	13	12	-	1	8	6	2	-	-	-	-	-
1962	47	41	4	2	28	26	2	-	19	15	2	2	-	-	-	-
1961	42	33	8	1	20	18	1	1	22	15	7	-	-	-	-	-
1960	56	44	8	4	21	18	-	3	35	26	8	1	-	-	-	-
1959	49	41	8	-	16	15	1	-	33	26	7	-	-	-	-	-
1958	49	41	7	1	20	20	-	-	28	20	7	1	1	1	-	-
1957	65	54	10	1	34	32	2	-	31	22	8	1	-	-	-	-
1956	65	52	12	1	21	20	-	1	43	31	12	-	1	1	-	-
1955	76	65	7	4	44	41	1	2	32	24	6	2	-	-	-	-
1954	81	71	9	1	38	37	1	-	42	33	8	1	1	1	-	-
1953	62	51	7	4	30	25	1	4	31	25	6	-	1	1	-	-
1952	83	71	12	-	36	35	1	-	47	36	11	-	-	-	-	-
1951	105	87	17	1	57	55	2	-	47	31	15	1	1	1	-	-
1950	82	68	13	1	40	36	4	-	42	32	9	1	-	-	-	-
1949	119	107	10	2	50	49	-	1	67	56	10	1	2	2	-	-
1948	119	95	22	2	35	32	1	2	82	61	21	-	2	2	-	-
1947	153	129	23	1	42	40	2	-	111	89	21	1	-	-	-	-
1946	131	107	22	2	46	45	-	1	84	61	22	1	1	1	-	-
1945	117	90	26	1	41	37	4	-	75	52	22	1	1	1	-	-
1944	120	96	24	-	47	45	2	-	70	48	22	-	3	3	-	-
1943	131	118	13	-	54	54	-	-	74	63	11	-	3	1	2	-
1942	147	115	25	7	67	57	4	6	80	58	21	1	-	-	-	-
1941	123	102	20	1	59	55	4	-	63	46	16	1	1	1	-	-
1940	124	105	15	4	49	44	2	3	75	61	13	1	-	-	-	-
1939	160	145	12	3	80	79	-	1	77	63	12	2	3	3	-	-
1938	190	154	25	11	96	89	1	6	92	63	24	5	2	2	-	-
1937	147	133	13	1	69	67	2	-	74	62	11	1	4	4	-	-
1936	195	181	10	4	92	86	2	4	101	93	8	-	2	2	-	-
1935	199	184	13	2	119	115	2	2	77	66	11	-	3	3	-	-
1934	168	154	14	-	65	64	1	-	102	89	13	-	1	1	-	-
1933	160	151	7	2	77	75	1	1	81	74	6	1	2	2	-	-
1932	140	128	10	2	62	62	-	-	75	63	10	2	3	3	-	-
1931	153	137	15	1	77	76	1	-	72	57	14	1	4	4	-	-
1930	155	147	6	2	90	90	-	-	65	57	6	2	-	-	-	-

[a] Includes 25 executed for armed robbery, 20 for kidnaping, 11 for burglary, 6 for sabotage, 6 for aggravated assault, and 2 for espionage.
[b] There were no executions from 1968 through 1976.

Source: U.S. Department of Justice, Bureau of Justice Statistics, *Correctional Populations in the United States, 1993*, NCJ-156241 (Washington, DC: U.S. Department of Justice, 1995), Table 7.26. Table adapted by SOURCEBOOK staff.

Source: Kathleen Maguire and Ann L. Pastore, eds., *Sourcebook of Criminal Justice Statistics — 1994*, U.S. Department of Justice, Bureau of Justice Statistics, Washington, DC; USGPO, 1995

TABLE 6.6

execution update

Total number of executions since the 1976 reinstatement of capital punishment (there were no executions in 1976):
302

'77	'78	'79	'80	'81	'82	'83	'84	'85	'86	'87	'88	'89	'90	'91	'92	'93	'94	'95
1	0	2	0	1	2	5	21	18	18	25	11	16	23	14	31	38	31	45

gender of defendants executed
total number 302

Female	1	(.33%)
Male	301	(99.67%)

gender of victims
total number 408

Female	181	(44.36%)
Male	227	(55.64%)

race of defendants executed

White	166	(54.97%)
Black	119	(39.40%)
Latino	16	(5.30%)
Native American	1	(.33%)

race of victims

White	337	(82.60%)
Black	52	(12.74%)
Latino	14	(3.43%)
Asian	5	(1.22%)

defendant-victim racial combinations

White Defendant and

White Victim	234	(57.35%)
Black Victim	4	(.98%)
Asian Victim	2	(.49%)
Latino/a Victim	5	(1.22%)

Black Defendant and

White Victim	96	(23.53%)
Black Victim	47	(11.52%)
Asian Victim	2	(.49%)
Latino Victim	1	(.24%)

Latino Defendant and

White Victim	8	(1.96%)
Latino Victim	7	(1.71%)
Asian Victim	1	(.24%)

Native American and

White Victim	1	(.24%)

Source: "Death Row USA," NAACP Legal Defense and Education Fund, Inc., New York City, Fall 1995

TABLE 6.7

PRISONERS EXECUTED UNDER CIVIL AUTHORITIES IN THE UNITED STATES, BY YEAR, RACE AND OFFENSE*

YEAR	TOTAL	WHITE	BLACK	HISPANIC	NATIVE AMERICAN
1990	23	16	7	0	0
1991	14	5	8	1	0
1992	31	19	10	2	0
1993	38	19	14	4	1
1994	31	19	11	1	0
1995**	45	22	19	1	0

*All were executed for the crime of murder.

**As of 10/31/95, race of one defendant was not identified
Source: Updated by staff of Information Plus from "Death Row USA," Fall 1995, prepared by the NAACP Legal Defense and Education Fund, Inc.

RACE AND ETHNICITY

More than half of those executed between 1930 and 1993 were Black (53 percent), 46 percent were White, and 1 percent were categorized as "other." (See Table 6.5.) Of the 302 prisoners executed from 1977 through October 1995, 55 percent were White (166), 39 percent were Black (119), 5 percent were Hispanic (16) and 0.33 percent were Native American (1). (See Table 6.6.)

Of the 31 executions carried out in 1994, 15 were non-Hispanic Whites. There were also 11 non-Hispanic Blacks, 1 White Hispanic, 1 White with unknown Hispanic origin, and 1 Black with unknown Hispanic origin. Of the 45 executions from January through October 1995, the NAACP Legal Defense Fund broke down the categories as follows: 22 Whites, 21 Blacks, 1 Hispanic, and one unidentified. (See Tables 6.6 and 6.7.)

The NAACP Legal Defense Fund keeps statistics not only on the race of the executed prisoners, but also on their victims. These statistics were used in court cases to decide

TABLE 6.8

Executions, by State and method, 1977-94

State	Number executed	Lethal injection	Electro-cution	Lethal gas	Firing squad	Hanging
Total	257	131	114	9	1	2
Texas	85	85				
Florida	33		33			
Virginia	24		24			
Louisiana	21	1	20			
Georgia	18		18			
Missouri	11	11				
Alabama	10		10			
Arkansas	9	8	1			
North Carolina	6	5		1		
Nevada	5	4		1		
Delaware	4	4				
Mississippi	4			4		
South Carolina	4		4			
Utah	4	3			1	
Arizona	3	2		1		
Indiana	3		3			
Oklahoma	3	3				
California	2			2		
Illinois	2	2				
Washington	2					2
Idaho	1	1				
Maryland	1	1				
Nebraska	1		1			
Wyoming	1	1				

Source: *Capital Punishment 1994*, Bureau of Justice Statistics, Washington, DC, 1996

CRIMES COMMITTED

The vast majority of executions from 1930 through 1993 were for murder (87 percent), followed by rape (11 percent) (Table 6.5). Rape is no longer punishable by death and the last execution for rape occurred in 1964. The Supreme Court had ruled in 1977 that rape did not warrant the death penalty (see Chapter III). However, a recent Louisiana law allows the death penalty in rape cases if the victim is less than 12 years old. This law has not yet been brought before the courts.

The remaining 2 percent of executions included 25 for armed robbery, 20 for kidnaping, 11 for burglary, 6 for sabotage, 6 for aggravated assault, and 2 for espionage. Since 1964, all those executed have been convicted on murder charges.

the constitutionality of the death penalty. The courts had to consider whether Whites who murdered Blacks got lighter sentences than Blacks who murdered Whites and whether those sentences violated the equal protection rights of the Constitution. (See Chapter IV for the outcome of these cases.)

From 1977 through October 1995, 57 percent of those executed were Whites who had murdered other Whites while less than 1 percent were Whites who had murdered Black persons. Twenty-three percent of those executed were Blacks who had murdered Whites, and 11.5 percent were Blacks who had murdered other Blacks. (See Table 6.6.)

METHOD OF EXECUTION

Among the 257 prisoners executed between 1977 and 1994, the largest number (131) received lethal injections, followed by those who were electrocuted (114). Nine executions were carried out by lethal gas, 2 by hanging, and 1 by firing squad. Texas, the state with the largest number of prisoners executed, used lethal injection in all of its 85 cases, while Florida used electrocution to execute its 33 prisoners. (See Table 6.8.)

CHAPTER VII

UNDER SENTENCE OF DEATH*

AN EVER-INCREASING NUMBER

In 1994, the Bureau of Justice Statistics reported a total of 2,890 prisoners held under sentence of death — a 5.9 percent increase over the previous year. The number of prisoners on death row has been increasing for more than 15 years (Figure 7.1). All prisoners under sentence of death on December 31, 1994, were convicted of murder. The continually growing number of prisoners on death row reflects a rise in the number of death sentences given, long stays on death row because of lengthy appeals, and the small number removed from death row for reasons other than execution (commutation, sentence overturned, natural death, murder, or suicide). However, many inmates have exhausted their appeals, and the number of executions likely will be increasing.

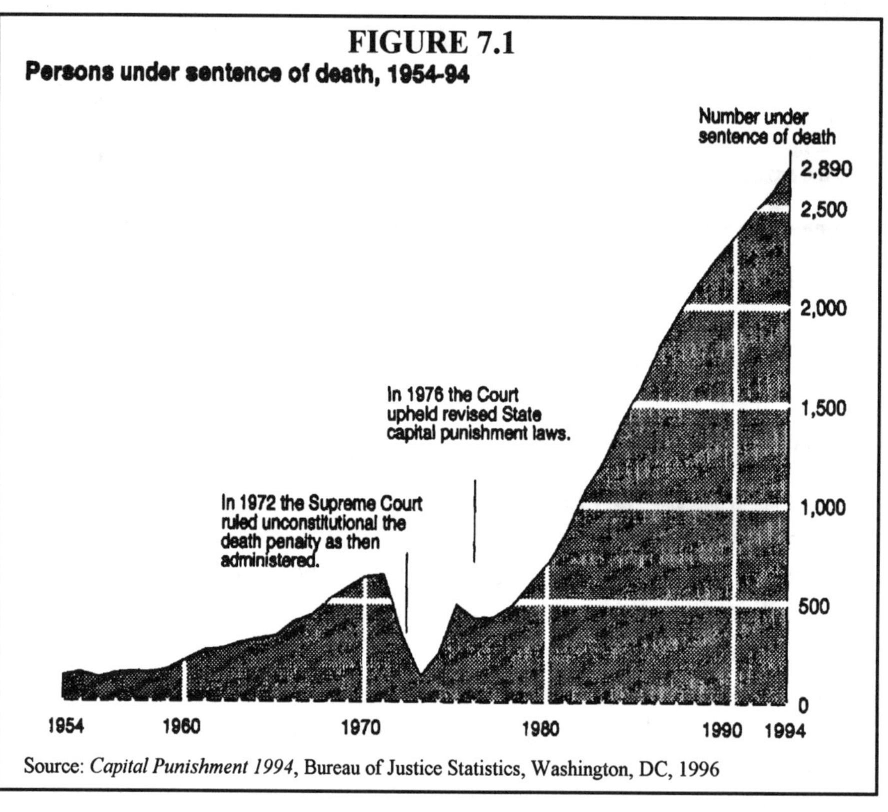

Source: *Capital Punishment 1994*, Bureau of Justice Statistics, Washington, DC, 1996

From 1973 to 1994, 5,280 persons received the death penalty. Of these, 257 were executed, 1,851 had their sentences or convictions overturned, 128 had their sentences commuted, and 125 died while waiting on death row. Over half (55 percent) are still on death row awaiting execution. (See Table 7.1.) During 1994, 304 prisoners under sentence of death went to state

---

*Statistical information on capital punishment mainly comes from two different sources that update their material at varying times. The Bureau of Statistics *Capital Punishment 1994* (Washington, DC, February 1996) gives information through 1994, and the Legal Defense Fund, a non-profit organization that collects information on capital punishment, publishes a quarterly release, "Death Row," the latest of which offers information through October 1995.

	Total sentenced to death, 1973-94	Number of removals, 1973-94					Under sentence of death, 12/31/94
State		Executed	Died	Sentence or conviction overturned	Sentence commuted	Other removals	
U.S. total	5,280	257	125	1,851	128	29	2,890
Federal	7	0	0	1	0	0	6
Alabama	227	10	4	77	1	0	135
Arizona	191	3	5	60	1	1	121
Arkansas	73	9	1	27	0	0	36
California	534	2	21	114	15	1	381
Colorado	14	0	1	9	1	0	3
Connecticut	5	0	0	1	0	0	4
Delaware	31	4	0	13	0	0	14
Florida	702	33	18	289	18	2	342
Georgia	246	18	7	119	5	1	96
Idaho	32	1	1	11	0	0	19
Illinois	223	2	6	53	0	7	155
Indiana	80	3	1	27	0	2	47
Kentucky	58	0	1	27	1	0	29
Louisiana	142	21	3	64	6	1	47
Maryland	37	1	1	20	2	0	13
Massachusetts	4	0	0	2	2	0	0
Mississippi	132	4	1	74	0	3	50
Missouri	117	11	4	13	1	0	88
Montana	13	0	0	4	1	0	8
Nebraska	21	1	2	6	2	0	10
Nevada	95	5	3	18	3	0	66
New Jersey	38	0	1	20	0	8	9
New Mexico	23	0	0	16	5	0	2
New York	3	0	0	3	0	0	0
North Carolina	364	6	4	239	4	0	111
Ohio	280	0	5	126	9	0	140
Oklahoma	236	3	4	100	0	0	129
Oregon	35	0	0	18	0	0	17
Pennsylvania	244	0	7	54	1	0	182
Rhode Island	2	0	0	2	0	0	0
South Carolina	129	4	3	63	0	0	59
South Dakota	2	0	0	0	0	0	2
Tennessee	163	0	4	57	0	2	100
Texas	624	85	12	90	43	0	394
Utah	23	4	0	8	1	0	10
Virginia	96	24	3	7	6	1	55
Washington	25	2	1	12	0	0	10
Wyoming	9	1	1	7	0	0	0
Percent	100%	4.9	2.4	35.1	2.4	0.5	54.7

Note: For those persons sentenced to death more than once, the numbers are based on the most recent sentence to death.

Source: *Capital Punishment 1994*, Bureau of Justice Statistics, Washington, DC, 1996

In January 1995, the NAACP Legal Defense Fund (LDF) reported 2,976 prisoners under sentence of death. By October 1995, they reported 3,046 death-row inmates. LDF statistics are higher than Bureau of Justice Statistics findings because the LDF includes persons who have been sentenced to death and are awaiting transfer to prison, while the Bureau of Justice Statistics counts only those on death row awaiting execution.

GEOGRAPHIC DISTRIBUTION

More than half of the prisoners (56 percent) awaiting execution were in the South. An additional 22 percent were in Western states, 15 percent were in Midwestern states, and the Northeastern states of Connecticut, New Jersey, New Hampshire, and Pennsylvania held 7 percent. About 39 percent of the condemned were awaiting execution in three states: Texas (394), California (381), and Florida (342). Of the 38 jurisdictions with statutes authorizing the death penalty, New Hampshire and Wyoming had no one under a capital sentence, and Connecticut, South Dakota, New Mexico, and Colorado had 4

prison systems by court order, 100 prisoners had their death sentences overturned, 3 had their sentences commuted, and 12 died while under a death sentence.

or fewer. (See Tables 7.2 and 7.3.) Between January 1 and December 31, 1994, 26 state prisons received 304 prisoners under sentence of death. Texas (43), Florida (39), North Carolina (27), and Alabama (24) accounted for 44 percent of the inmates entering prisons under a death sentence during the year.

SEX AND RACE

Almost 99 percent of the 2,890 persons under sentence of death were males (Table 7.4). Only 41 females were awaiting execution in 1994, an increase of 5 from 1993. Of these, 27 were White and 14 were Black. According to the Legal Defense Fund, the 49 females who had been sentenced to death between 1973 and October 1995 were still on death row in October 1995, compared to 2,997 males.

Among those under sentence of death, the majority (57 percent) were White; 41 percent were Black. Hispanic prisoners (224), whose ethnicity was known and who may be of any race, accounted for 8 percent of those under a death sentence. (See Tables 7.4 and 7.5.) In 1994, more than three-fourths of the 224 Hispanics sentenced to death were in four states: Texas (63), California (55), Florida (32), and Arizona (20). According to the Legal Defense Fund, 1,476 Whites (48.46 percent), 1,235 Blacks (40.54) percent, 234 Hispanics (7.68 percent), 52 Native Americans (1.71 percent), and 24 Asians (0.79 percent) were under sentence of death as of October 1995.

CHARACTERISTICS OF PRISONERS

The median age of those under sentence of death in 1994 was nearly 35 years; more than 4 out of 10 (44 percent) were between 30 and 39 years old and 73 percent were age 25 to 44. Few were under 20 years old (0.7 percent) or over 55 years (3.3 percent). In 1994, the youngest was 17 years old, having been sentenced in November 1994 at the age of 17, and the oldest was 78, having been sentenced in June 1983 at the age of 68. More than half of all inmates under sentence of death at year-end 1994 were ages 20 to 29 when they were arrested for their capital offense. (See Table 7.6.)

Among those for whom information was available, more than half (52 percent) had not graduated from high school, and only one in 10 (10 percent) had any college education. The largest proportion had never married (50 percent), and more than 1 in 5 (21 percent) were separated or divorced. (See Table 7.4.)

CRIMINAL HISTORY OF DEATH ROW INMATES

Among prisoners on death row, 2 of 3 (67 percent) had prior felony convictions. Almost 1 in 11 (9 percent) had been previously convicted of murder or manslaughter. About 2 of 5 (42 percent) had an active criminal justice record at the time of the murder for which they were condemned. About half of those with an active criminal record were out on parole when they committed their crimes, and one-fourth were on probation. The others had charges pending, were in prison, had

TABLE 7.2

Status of the death penalty, December 31, 1994

Executions during 1994		Number of prisoners under sentence of death		Jurisdictions without a death penalty
Texas	14	Texas	394	Alaska
Arkansas	5	California	381	District of Columbia
Virginia	2	Florida	342	Hawaii
Delaware	1	Pennsylvania	182	Iowa
Florida	1	Illinois	155	Maine
Georgia	1	Ohio	140	Massachusetts
Idaho	1	Alabama	135	Michigan
Illinois	1	Oklahoma	129	Minnesota
Indiana	1	Arizona	121	New York
Maryland	1	North Carolina	111	North Dakota
Nebraska	1	Tennessee	100	Rhode Island
North Carolina	1	Georgia	96	Vermont
Washington	1	23 other jurisdictions	604	West Virginia
				Wisconsin
Total	31	Total	2,890	

Source: *Capital Punishment 1994*, Bureau of Justice Statistics, Washington, DC, 1996

TABLE 7.3

Prisoners under sentence of death, by region, State, and race, 1993 and 1994

Region and State	Prisoners under sentence of death, 12/31/93			Received under sentence of death			Removed from death row(excluding execution)[a]			Executed			Prisoners under sentence of death, 12/31/94		
	Total[b]	White[c]	Black[c]	Total[b]	White	Black	Total[b]	White	Black	Total[b]	White	Black	Total[b]	White	Black
U.S. total	2,729	1,577	1,111	304	160	136	112	72	39	31	20	11	2,890	1,645	1,197
Federal[d]	6	3	3	0	0	0	0	0	0	0	0	0	6	3	3
State	2,723	1,574	1,108	304	160	136	112	72	39	31	20	11	2,884	1,642	1,194
Northeast	180	68	107	24	7	15	9	3	6	0	0	0	195	72	116
Connecticut	5	3	2	0	0	0	1	1	0	0	0	0	4	2	2
New Hampshire	0	0	0	0	0	0	0	0	0	0	0	0	0	0	0
New Jersey	7	4	3	3	0	3	1	0	1	0	0	0	9	4	5
Pennsylvania	168	61	102	21	7	12	7	2	5	0	0	0	182	66	109
Midwest	420	207	211	36	19	17	11	8	3	3	1	2	442	217	223
Illinois	151	57	94	11	5	6	6	4	2	1	1	0	155	57	98
Indiana	47	31	16	2	1	1	1	1	0	1	0	1	47	31	16
Missouri	80	47	33	9	5	4	1	1	0	0	0	0	88	51	37
Nebraska	11	7	3	1	1	0	1	1	0	1	0	1	10	7	2
Ohio	129	63	65	13	7	6	2	1	1	0	0	0	140	69	70
South Dakota	2	2	0	0	0	0	0	0	0	0	0	0	2	2	0
South	1,512	882	610	195	103	89	71	46	24	26	17	9	1,610	922	686
Alabama	120	64	54	24	13	11	9	3	6	0	0	0	135	74	59
Arkansas	33	20	13	8	5	3	0	0	0	5	4	1	36	21	15
Delaware	15	7	8	0	0	0	0	0	0	1	0	1	14	7	7
Florida	325	208	117	39	23	16	21	16	5	1	1	0	342	214	128
Georgia	96	48	48	6	6	0	5	1	4	1	0	1	96	53	43
Kentucky	29	22	7	4	4	0	4	3	1	0	0	0	29	23	6
Louisiana	43	14	29	6	3	3	2	1	1	0	0	0	47	16	31
Maryland	14	3	11	0	0	0	0	0	0	1	1	0	13	2	11
Mississippi	50	20	30	5	2	3	5	2	3	0	0	0	50	20	30
North Carolina	99	55	42	27	11	15	14	10	3	1	1	0	111	55	54
Oklahoma	122	80	33	12	4	7	5	5	0	0	0	0	129	79	40
South Carolina	52	28	24	7	3	4	0	0	0	0	0	0	59	31	28
Tennessee	99	67	30	4	2	2	3	3	0	0	0	0	100	66	32
Texas	366	221	140	43	25	17	1	1	0	14	10	4	394	235	153
Virginia	49	25	24	10	2	8	2	1	1	2	0	2	55	26	29
West	611	417	180	49	31	15	21	15	6	2	2	0	637	431	189
Arizona	117	100	14	10	5	2	6	5	1	0	0	0	121	100	15
California	363	217	138	22	11	11	4	2	2	0	0	0	381	226	147
Colorado	3	3	0	0	0	0	0	0	0	0	0	0	3	3	0
Idaho	21	21	0	0	0	0	1	1	0	1	1	0	19	19	0
Montana	8	6	0	0	0	0	0	0	0	0	0	0	8	6	0
Nevada	64	41	23	8	7	1	6	3	3	0	0	0	66	45	21
New Mexico	1	1	0	1	1	0	0	0	0	0	0	0	2	2	0
Oregon	13	12	0	6	5	1	2	2	0	0	0	0	17	15	1
Utah	11	9	2	0	0	0	1	1	0	0	0	0	10	8	2
Washington	10	7	3	2	2	0	1	1	0	1	1	0	10	7	3
Wyoming	0	0	0	0	0	0	0	0	0	0	0	0	0	0	0

Note: States not listed and the District of Columbia did not authorize the death penalty as of 12/31/93. Some figures shown for yearend 1993 are revised from those reported in *Capital Punishment 1993* (NCJ-150042). The revised figures include 27 inmates who were either reported late to the National Prisoner Statistics Program or were not in custody of State correctional authorities on 12/31/93 (12 in Texas; 5 in Arizona; 3 in Florida; 2 each in Georgia and Illinois; and 1 each in California, North Carolina, and Tennessee), and exclude 19 inmates who were relieved of the death sentence on or before 12/31/93 (3 each in Illinois and Texas; 2 each in Florida, Georgia, and Louisiana; and 1 each in California, Idaho, Kentucky, Maryland, Nevada, North Carolina, and South Carolina).

[a]Includes 8 deaths from natural causes (3 in Florida, 2 in Arizona, and 1 each in California, Illinois, and Pennsylvania), 3 suicides (1 each in Alabama, California, and Florida), and 1 inmate shot to death by a correctional officer (California).

[b]Totals include persons of other races.

[c]The accounting of race and Hispanic origin differs from that presented in tables   In this table white and black inmates include Hispanics.

[d]Excludes persons held under Armed Forces jurisdiction with a military death sentence for murder.

Source: *Capital Punishment 1994*, Bureau of Justice Statistics, Washington, DC, 1996

TABLE 7.4

Demographic characteristics of prisoners under sentence of death, 1994

Characteristic	Prisoners under sentence of death, 1994		
	Yearend	Admissions	Removals
Total number under sentence of death	2,890	304	143
Sex			
Male	98.6%	98.4%	100%
Female	1.4	1.6	0
Race			
White	56.9%	52.6%	64.3%
Black	41.4	44.7	35.0
Other*	1.7	2.6	.7
Hispanic origin			
Hispanic	8.4%	10.3%	7.6%
Non-Hispanic	91.6	89.7	92.4
Education			
8th grade or less	15.3%	17.1%	22.1%
9th–11th	37.1	34.9	34.4
High school graduate/GED	37.4	37.0	29.8
Any college	10.2	11.0	13.7
Median	12th grade	12th grade	11th grade
Marital status			
Married	26.6%	25.0%	30.4%
Divorced/separated	21.3	16.8	20.0
Widowed	2.5	1.5	4.0
Never married	49.6	56.7	45.6

Note: Calculations are based on those cases for which data were reported. Missing data by category were as follows:

	Yearend	Admissions	Removals
Hispanic origin	237	63	12
Education	381	58	11
Marital status	228	37	18

*At yearend 1993 "other" consisted of 22 Native Americans, 16 Asians, and 3 self-identified Hispanics. During 1994, 2 Native Americans, 1 Asian, and 5 self-identified Hispanics were admitted, and 1 Native American was removed.

TABLE 7.5

Hispanics and women under sentence of death, by State, 1993 and 1994

	Under sentence of death, 12/31/93		Received under sentence of death		Death sentence removed*	Under sentence of death, 12/31/94	
	Hispanics	Women	Hispanics	Women	Hispanics	Hispanics	Women
U.S. Total	209	36	25	5	9	224	41
Alabama	0	4	0	1	0	0	5
Arizona	20	1	1	0	1	20	1
Arkansas	1	0	0	0	0	1	0
California	52	4	3	2	0	55	6
Colorado	1	0	0	0	0	1	0
Florida	31	4	5	0	4	32	4
Georgia	1	0	0	0	0	1	0
Idaho	2	1	0	0	0	2	1
Illinois	9	4	0	1	1	8	5
Indiana	2	0	0	0	0	2	0
Mississippi	1	1	0	0	0	1	1
Missouri	0	2	0	0	0	0	2
Nevada[b]	7	1	1	0	0	8	1
New Jersey	1	0	0	0	0	1	0
New Mexico	0	0	1	0	0	1	0
North Carolina	2	2	0	0	2	0	2
Ohio	5	0	0	0	0	5	0
Oklahoma	6	4	0	0	0	6	4
Oregon	1	0	0	0	0	1	0
Pennsylvania	7	3	4	1	0	11	4
Tennessee	1	1	0	0	0	1	1
Texas	55	4	10	0	1	63	4
Utah	2	0	0	0	0	2	0
Virginia	2	0	0	0	0	2	0

*No women were removed from under sentence of death or executed during 1994. One Hispanic was executed in Texas in 1994.

[b]Preliminary data, subject to revision.

Source of both tables: *Capital Punishment 1994*, Bureau of Justice Statistics, Washington, DC, 1996

---

escaped from incarceration, or had some other criminal justice status. (See Table 7.7.)

Since 1988, data have been collected on the number of death sentences imposed on entering inmates. Among the 1,976 individuals received under sentence of death from 1988 to 1994, about 1 in every 7 entered with two or more death sentences (Table 7.8).

Criminal history patterns varied slightly by race and Hispanic origin. Blacks (71.5 percent) had somewhat more prior felony convictions than Whites (65 percent) and Hispanics (60 percent). About the same proportion of Blacks (9 percent), Whites (8 percent), and Hispanics (8 percent) had a prior homicide conviction. A somewhat higher proportion of Hispanics (27 percent) than Whites (17 percent) or Blacks (23 percent) were on parole when arrested for their capital offense. (See Table 7.7.)

A LONG WAIT

It can be a long wait on death row. Between 1977 and 1994, a total of 4,937 offenders had been under a death sentence for varying periods. Of these, 257 (5.2 percent) were actually executed (Table 7.9). Another 1,790 (36.2 percent) were removed from under a death sentence by appellate court decisions and reviews, commutations, or death. For those executed since 1977, the average time between the imposition

TABLE 7.6

Demographic characteristics of prisoners under sentence of death, 1994

Characteristic	Prisoners under sentence of death, 1994		
	Yearend	Admissions	Removals
Total number under sentence of death	2,890	304	143
Sex			
Male	98.6%	98.4%	100%
Female	1.4	1.6	0
Race			
White	56.9%	52.6%	64.3%
Black	41.4	44.7	35.0
Other*	1.7	2.6	.7
Hispanic origin			
Hispanic	8.4%	10.3%	7.6%
Non-Hispanic	91.6	89.7	92.4
Education			
8th grade or less	15.3%	17.1%	22.1%
9th–11th	37.1	34.9	34.4
High school graduate/GED	37.4	37.0	29.8
Any college	10.2	11.0	13.7
Median	12th grade	12th grade	11th grade
Marital status			
Married	26.6%	25.0%	30.4%
Divorced/separated	21.3	16.8	20.0
Widowed	2.5	1.5	4.0
Never married	49.6	56.7	45.6

Note: Calculations are based on those cases for which data were reported. Missing data by category were as follows:

	Yearend	Admissions	Removals
Hispanic origin	237	63	12
Education	381	58	11
Marital status	228	37	18

*At yearend 1993 "other" consisted of 22 Native Americans, 18 Asians, and 3 self-identified Hispanics. During 1994, 2 Native Americans, 1 Asian, and 5 self-identified Hispanics were admitted, and 1 Native American was removed.

TABLE 7.7

Criminal history profile of prisoners under sentence of death by race and Hispanic origin, 1994

	Prisoners under sentence of death							
	Number				Percent[a]			
	All races[b]	White	Black	Hispanic	All races[b]	White	Black	Hispanic
U.S. total	2,890	1,441	1,185	224	100.0%	100.0%	100.0%	100.0%
Prior felony convictions								
Yes	1,810	878	791	124	67.1%	65.1%	71.5%	59.6%
No	889	471	315	84	32.9	34.9	28.5	40.4
Not reported	191	92	79	16				
Prior homicide convictions								
Yes	243	116	108	17	8.6%	8.2%	9.4%	7.8%
No	2,576	1,293	1,046	200	91.4	91.8	90.6	92.2
Not reported	71	32	31	7				
Legal status at time of capital offense								
Charges pending	175	95	64	13	6.8%	7.4%	6.1%	6.6%
Probation	251	124	104	20	9.8	9.6	10.0	10.2
Parole	518	216	245	53	20.2	16.9	23.4	26.9
Prison escapee	42	25	13	3	1.6	1.9	1.2	1.5
Prison inmate	61	31	27	3	2.4	2.4	2.6	1.5
Other status	31	15	14	1	1.2	1.2	1.3	0.5
None	1,487	779	580	104	58.0	60.6	55.4	52.8
Not reported	325	156	138	27				

[a]Percentages are based on those offenders for whom data were reported.

[b]Includes whites, blacks, Hispanics, and persons of other races.

Source of both tables: *Capital Punishment 1994*, Bureau of Justice Statistics, Washington, DC, 1996

Of the 2,890 persons under sentence of death on December 31, 1994, 99 (3.4 percent) were sentenced prior to 1980. Florida, Texas, California, and Georgia housed the inmates who had served the longest among all condemned inmates. By contrast Connecticut and Oregon, had no inmates sentenced prior to 1989, the federal prison system had none sentenced prior to 1991, and South Dakota had none sentenced before 1992. By December 31, 1994, the average time spent under sentence of death for the 2,890

TABLE 7.8

Number of death sentences received	Inmates
Total	100 %
1	86.0
2	9.8
3 or more	4.3
Number admitted under sentence of death, 1988-94	1,976

Source: *Capital Punishment 1994*, Bureau of Justice Statistics, Washington, DC, 1996

condemned inmates was 6.3 years. (See Table 7.11.)

GETTING OFF DEATH ROW

Table 7.12 shows the means by which prisoners can get off death row. The table breaks down the outcome of the sentences for those condemned to death row for the period 1973 through 1994. During this period, 257 (5 percent) were actually executed. The overwhelming majority of those who left death row got off because of an appeals court action. Some (128) had their sentences commuted, while another 125 died while on death row.

Using a single year as an example, of the 295 persons who were sentenced to death in 1988, 8 have been executed, 6 died while in confinement, 66 had their convictions or sentences overturned (conviction and sentencing are two separate trials under the bifurcated [two part] system required in death-penalty cases). Of the 295 prisoners sentenced in 1988, 214 were still on death row on December 31, 1992.

AUTOMATIC REVIEW

At year-end 1994, of the 37 states with capital punishment statutes, 36 provided for review of all death sentences regardless of the defendants' wishes. Arkansas had no specific provisions for automatic review, and the issue was in litigation in South Carolina. The federal death-penalty procedures do not provide for automatic review after a sentence of

death is imposed. While most of the 36 states authorize an automatic review of both conviction and sentence, Idaho, Indiana, Montana, Oklahoma, and Tennessee require review of the sentence only. In Idaho, review of the conviction must be appealed or forfeited (if the defendant does not appeal his conviction, his right to do so is waived). In Indiana, a defendant may waive review of the conviction.

The review is usually conducted by the state's highest appellate court, regardless of the defendant's wishes. If either the conviction or the sentence is overturned, the case may be remanded (returned) to the trial court for additional proceedings or for retrial. As a result of retrial or resentencing, the death sentence may be reinstated.

With the growing numbers, death-row inmates are finding it more difficult to get lawyers to help with their appeals. Most states require poorer defendants to be supplied with lawyers for their initial appeals, but after that the prisoner must get his or her own counsel. Since most of those awaiting execution are poor, they must find lawyers willing to handle appeals on a *pro bono* (for free) basis. With the growing numbers of condemned, organizations that help prisoners get

TABLE 7.9

Prisoners under sentence of death who were executed or received other dispositions, by race and Hispanic origin, 1977-94

Race and Hispanic origin[b]	Total under sentence of death, 1977-94[c]	Prisoners executed		Prisoners who received other dispositions[a]	
		Number	Percent of total	Number	Percent of total
All races or ethnic groups	4,937	257	5.2%	1,790	36.2%
White	2,521	140	5.6	940	37.3
Black	2,018	98	4.9	735	36.4
Hispanic	331	17	5.1	90	27.2
Other	67	2	3.0	25	37.3

[a]Includes persons removed from a sentence of death because of statutes struck down on appeal, sentences or convictions vacated, commutations, or death other than by execution.
[b]White, black, and other categories exclude Hispanics.
[c]Includes persons sentenced to death prior to 1977 who were still under sentence of death 12/31/94 (16), persons sentenced to death prior to 1977 whose death sentence was removed between 1977 and 12/31/94 (364), and persons sentenced to death between 1977 and 12/31/94 (4,557).

Source: *Capital Punishment 1994*, Bureau of Justice Statistics, Washington, DC, 1996

TABLE 7.10

Time under sentence of death sentence and execution, by race, 1977-94

Year of execution	Number executed			Average elapsed time from sentence to execution for:		
	All races*	White	Black	All races*	White	Black
Total	257	156	99	97 mos	92 mos	106 mos
1977-83	11	9	2	51 mos	49 mos	58 mos
1984	21	13	8	74	76	71
1985	18	11	7	71	65	80
1986	18	11	7	87	78	102
1987	25	13	12	86	78	96
1988	11	6	5	80	72	89
1989	16	8	8	95	78	112
1990	23	16	7	95	97	91
1991	14	7	7	116	124	107
1992	31	19	11	114	104	135
1993	38	23	14	113	112	121
1994	31	20	11	122	117	132

Note: Average time was calculated from the most recent sentencing date. Some numbers have been revised from those previously reported. *Includes Native Americans.

Source: *Capital Punishment 1994*, Bureau of Justice Statistics, Washington, DC, 1996

legal counsel are finding it more difficult to locate enough lawyers willing to work for free.

The Legal Services Corporation, created in 1974 to provide grants to non-profit legal providers, received only $278 million in the 1996 federal budget, compared with $400 million in 1995. The conservative Republican-dominated Congress, claiming the money is being used for political purposes rather than legal objectives, wants to limit the power of the organization which provides legal assistance to the poor. These grants include money for death-penalty resource centers which provide lawyers for death-row inmates. Due to the cuts, many of these centers do not have enough money to operate and have shut down.

Lawyers defending condemned prisoners often receive the case within a few months or weeks of the scheduled execution and, knowing little about the case, search through the case for what are often considered "technicalities" in order to gain delays and stays of execution so they can then handle the case properly.

JAMMING THE COURT DOCKETS

The Supreme Court has become increasingly impatient with the issue of delays due to the number of appeals. In 1987, the High Court ruled, in *McCleskey v. Kemp* (481 US 279), that broad-based scientific findings of racial discrimination were not a defense and that a claim of racial discrimination had to apply to the particular case being considered. (See Chapter IV.) Many observers consider this case to be the last systemic challenge to the death penalty on federal constitutional grounds — that the death penalty was a violation of the prisoner's constitutional rights of either equal protection or the issue of cruel and unusual punishment.

With the conservative majority on the Supreme Court, this is unlikely to change. This situation has forced lawyers defending condemned prisoners to stress procedural grounds. Currently, according to the Bureau of Justice Statistics, it takes about 8 years, 1 month from the imposition of the death sentence until execution.

EXECUTING THE INNOCENT

The change in emphasis away from constitutional issues has also led some to investigate the issue of guilt and innocence. While the overwhelming majority of those sentenced to death are unquestionably guilty of murder, a small fraction have been wrongly convicted. Hugo Bedau of Tufts University (Massachusetts) and Michael Radelet of the University of Florida, in *Miscarriages of Justice in Potentially Capital Cases* (1985), counted, since the turn of the century, 343 cases in which a defendant facing a possible death penalty was wrongfully convicted. Of these, 137 were sentenced to death and 25 were actually executed. Sixty-one served more than 10 years in jail, and 7 died in prison.

James Marquart and Jonathan Sorensen, both of Sam Houston State University (Texas), in an unpublished study, traced the lives of 558 death-row inmates whose executions were commuted to prison terms by the 1972 Supreme Court decisions. Four were later released as innocent, four others murdered again while in prison, and another, following his release, killed again before committing suicide. The researchers claim that "executing all of them would not have greatly protected society. We would have executed nearly 600 convicts to protect us from five. And we would have killed four innocent people in the process."

THE COST OF AN EXECUTION

Some abolitionists have advocated life imprisonment without the chance of parole as an alternative to the death sentence. According to the Bureau of Justice Statistics, the average murderer sentenced to life with a chance of parole serves 71 months *(Prison Sentences and Time Served for Violence,* Washington, DC, 1995). (See Table 7.13.) While a 1991 Gallup Poll still found a majority of Americans (53 percent) continuing to

TABLE 7.12

**Prisoners sentenced to death, and the outcome of their sentence,
by year of sentencing, 1973-94**

Year of sentence	Number sentenced to death	Execution	Other death	Appeal or higher courts overturned — Death penalty statute	Conviction	Sentence	Sentence commuted	Other or unknown reasons	Under sentence of death, 12/31/94
1973	42	2	0	14	9	8	9	0	0
1974	149	9	4	65	15	29	22	1	4
1975	298	5	4	171	24	66	21	2	5
1976	234	11	5	137	16	43	15	0	7
1977	138	16	2	40	26	33	7	0	14
1978	187	29	3	21	35	60	8	0	31
1979	156	15	8	2	28	58	6	1	38
1980	182	20	11	3	31	47	6	0	64
1981	233	31	10	0	40	68	4	1	79
1982	272	33	12	0	28	63	6	0	130
1983	253	26	10	1	19	48	4	2	143
1984	287	21	10	2	33	55	6	8	152
1985	277	7	3	2	31	63	3	3	165
1986	306	9	12	0	40	49	4	5	187
1987	290	3	7	2	32	52	1	6	187
1988	295	8	6	0	24	42	1	0	214
1989	264	3	6	0	21	48	3	0	183
1990	256	3	3	0	25	28	0	0	197
1991	277	1	4	0	16	16	0	0	240
1992	285	4	1	0	11	8	1	0	260
1993	295	1	4	0	1	2	0	0	287
1994	304	0	0	0	0	0	1	0	303
Total, 1973-94	5,280	257	125	460	505	886	128	29	2,890

Note: Table based upon most recent death sentence received.

Source: *Capital Punishment 1994*, Bureau of Justice Statistics, Washington, DC, 1996

favor the death penalty over life without parole (35 percent — see Chapter VIII), this alternative of sentencing murders to life without parole may have simply come about because it has become so expensive to execute a prisoner. Ronald M. George, a justice on the California Supreme Court, commented that "it certainly is an expensive process. It has to be, in order to make it fair." Franklin E. Zimring, director of the Earl Warren Legal Institute at the University of California at Berkeley, maintained that "It is always more expensive to have and use the death penalty than it is not to have it, for the very simple reason that lawyers are more expensive than prison guards."

Various Estimates

A study of the California system suggested a minimum cost of $500,000 per case (this includes all capital cases, not just the ones where the cases end with a death sentence). In 1994, California set up the Office of Public Defender which works exclusively on appeals for poor defendants on death row at an annual cost of $8 million. Because the office cannot handle all the defendants, the state offers private attorneys contracts for $75,000 to $200,000 to handle cases. Despite these efforts, about one-third of the prisoners on death row do not have lawyers to represent them in the appeals process. Many death-penalty cases are on hold because lawyers cannot be found to handle the appeals.

In a lecture at Case Western Reserve Law School (1995), Alex Kozinski, a judge on the United States Court of Appeals for the Ninth Circuit, estimated that death penalty cases cost taxpayers about one million dollars more than

TABLE 7.13			
Released violent offenders in 1992 served 48% of their sentence			
Type of offense	Average sentence	Average time served*	Percent of sentence served
All violent	89 months	43 months	48%
Homicide	149	71	48
Rape	117	65	56
Kidnaping	104	52	50
Robbery	95	44	46
Sexual assault	72	35	49
Assault	61	29	48
Other	60	28	47

*Includes jail credit and prison time.

Source: *Prison Sentences and Time Served for Violence*, Bureau of Justice Statistics, Washington, DC, 1995

non-capital cases. He claimed that California spent $90 million annually on capital-punishment cases. When a case enters the federal system, the United States pays for indigent defense. In one federal district court, the defense received $400,000, a sum that did not include the appeal to the Supreme Court.

A study in New York State estimated the cost per capital case at $1.8 million, while a Maryland study figured about $750,000 per case. A 1991 study of the Texas criminal justice system estimated the cost of appealing capital murder cases at $2,316,655. Some expenses included $265,640 for the trial; $294,240 for the state appeals; $113,608 for federal appeals (over six years); and $135,875 for death-row housing. In contrast, the cost of housing a prisoner in a Texas maximum security prison single cell for 40 years was $750,000. Many small Texas counties stopped asking for the death penalty because it was too expensive.

A 1993 Duke University study (*Costs of Processing Murder Cases in North Carolina*), prepared by Phillip J. Cook and Donna B. Slawson, professors of public policy at Duke, studied the total costs of every death penalty case in the state over two years. They found that, in North Carolina, the cost to try a non-capital murder case and imprison a convicted murderer for 20 years was $166,000. The cost to try a capital murder case, convict, and execute a prisoner after ten years of imprisonment averaged $329,000. A non-capital murder case thus saved the state and local governments an estimated $163,000.

However, only one-third (31 percent) of the capital murder trials resulted in a sentence of death. Only about 10 percent of those condemned to death were actually executed. Many of those sentenced to death had retrials or new sentencing trials which had different results than their original trials. Cook and Slawson estimated that the extra cost for each case in which the defendant was sentenced to death was about $216,000, and the extra cost per case in which the defendant was executed was more than $2.16 million.

Some of the costs involved in a capital murder case that might not be involved in a non-capital murder trial in North Carolina included indigent defendants who have the right to two lawyers instead of one, more expert witnesses, and more briefs filed. The appeals process has nine steps, some of which can be repeated.

Other Cost Concerns

Introducing life imprisonment without parole would probably require a huge prison construction program. In 1993, according to the Edna McConnell Clark Foundation (an advocacy group which seeks "a more rational, humane, and effective criminal justice system"), the costs of construction averaged $78,000 per bed for federal penitentiaries and $54,209 per bed for state prisons. Currently, building one prison cell costs approximately $100,000 without considering the interest paid on the bonds passed for prison construction. The Criminal Justice Institute (Camille Graham Camp and George M. Camp, *The Corrections Yearbook — Adult Corrections*, South Salem, NY, 1994) estimated that the states spent a daily average of $52.38 per inmate in 1993 (more than $19,000 annually).

The cost of executing a convicted murderer can also be counted in ways other than dollars. A Texas spokesperson for VOTERS (Victims

Organized to Ensure Rights and Safety) commented that only in rare cases does the organization support the death penalty over life without parole. Because the process is so long and difficult, the family of the murder victim is required to relive their nightmare many times at each appeal, each hearing, and each scheduled execution date.

Supporters of the death penalty point out that they advocate proper review of the cases. However, they stress that both the lengthy time and the high expense resulting from innumerable appeals, many over "technicalities" which have little or nothing to do with the question of guilt or innocence, do little more than jam up the nation's court system. If these "frivolous" appeals were eliminated, the procedure would neither take so long nor cost so much.

FAIRNESS AND THE DEATH PENALTY

Racial Questions

Death penalty cases raise a fairness issue. Opponents to the death penalty claim that minorities and poor defendants are more likely to be convicted and receive the death penalty than White and wealthy defendants. On appeal, the lawyers for Warren McCleskey, a convicted murderer, brought before the Supreme Court the Baldus study, an analysis of 600 cases in Georgia in the 1970s. This study showed that Black defendants who were convicted of killing Whites were more likely to receive death sentences than White murderers or than Black murderers who killed Black victims. The justices, in *McCleskey v. Kemp* (481 US 279, 1987) rejected the study, declaring that "apparent disparities ... are an inevitable part of our criminal justice system" and that there were enough safeguards built into the legal system to protect every defendant. (See Chapter IV.)

In 1990, the General Accounting Office (GAO) of the federal government reviewed 28 studies on race and the death penalty. The GAO found that "in 82 percent of the studies, the race of the victim was found to influence the likelihood of being charged with capital murder or receiving the death penalty." When the victim was White, the defendant, White or Black, was more likely to get the death sentence. The studies showed that for crimes of passion, the convicted rarely received the death penalty, and in the small number of horrendous murders, death sentences were more likely imposed, regardless of race. However, in cases such as killing someone while robbing him or when the murderer had a previous record, the race of the victim played a role.

About half the people murdered each year are Black, but according to the NAACP Legal Defense Fund (an organization that opposes capital punishment and monitors capital punishment statistics), from 1977 to August 31, 1995, the victims of those executed for murder were 12.9 percent Black and 82.3 percent White. Because of these statistics, anti-capital punishment groups have unsuccessfully tried to get Congress to pass racial justice provisions to federal laws which would require quantitative studies of racial disparities in capital punishment sentencing cases.

Stephen P. Klein, a researcher at the Rand Corporation, a think tank, does not believe these studies prove bias. He believes that the study methods used could not show cause and effect and that the actual number of cases was too small to prove bias. He adds that there are many other factors, such as the believability of witnesses, that might affect the outcome of the trials. Dr. van den Haag, a death-penalty proponent (see Chapter X), commented that the research was unimportant. If discrimination exists, then he advised that the solution was not to abolish capital punishment, but to end the disparities and increase the number of executions of those who kill Blacks.

CHAPTER VIII

PUBLIC ATTITUDES TOWARDS CAPITAL PUNISHMENT

The majority of Americans strongly favors capital punishment. In fact, a 1994 poll prepared by the National Opinion Research Center of the University of Illinois (IL), a questionnaire by the Higher Educational Research Institute (CA), and a 1995 survey by Gallup Poll showed that 74 to 77 percent of Americans supported the death penalty for those convicted of murder.

TABLE 8.1

Do you favor or oppose the death penalty for persons convicted of murder?

[VAR: CAPPUN]

RESPONSE	PUNCH	1972-82	1982	1983-87	YEAR 1987	1988-91	1993	1994	COL. 360 ALL
Favor	1	6933	154	5410	154	4,274	1151	2215	20,291
Oppose	2	2936	165	1696	165	1,242	337	580	7,121
Don't know	8	607	32	399	33	364	112	184	1,731
No answer	9	33	3	37	1	27	6	13	120
Not applicable	BK	3117	0	0	0	0	0	0	3,117

Source: National Opinion Research Center, University of Chicago, December, 1994

SUPPORT INCREASING

Over the past dozen years, the National Opinion Research Center has reported an increase in support for capital punishment. Between 1972 and 1982, approximately 66 percent of those polled indicated they favored capital punishment for persons convicted of murder. This proportion rose to 72 percent in the years 1983 to 1987 and remained there for the rest of the 1980s and the early 1990s. In 1994, the National Research Center found that almost 3 out of 4 Americans (74 percent) supported capital punishment, while only about 1 in 5 (19 percent) opposed it (Table 8.1).

Gallup Poll findings mirror those of the National Opinion Research Center. A May 1995 poll, the most recent published by Gallup, found that 77 percent of Americans favored the death penalty, 13 percent opposed it, 8 percent said it depends, and 2 percent had no opinion about capital punishment as an option in murder cases (Figure 8.1). This finding is consistent with the steady growth in the support for capital punishment over the past 25 years (Table 8.2). The lowest proportion to support capital punishment

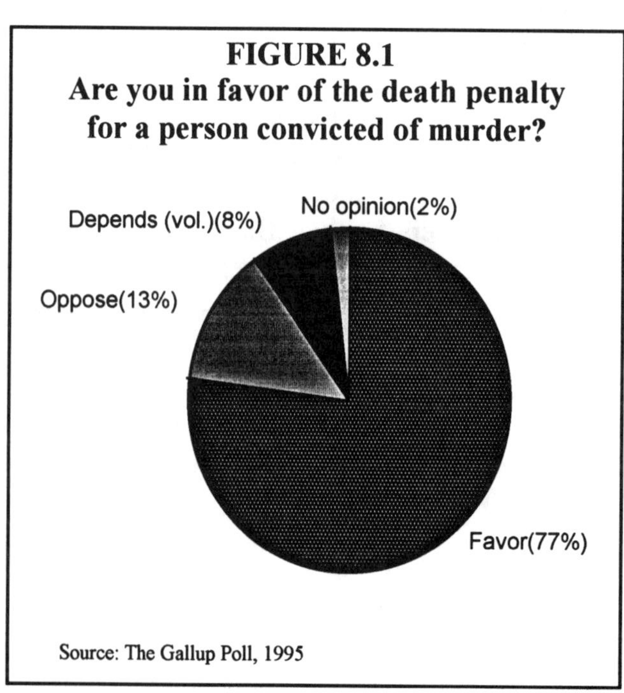

FIGURE 8.1
Are you in favor of the death penalty for a person convicted of murder?

Source: The Gallup Poll, 1995

TABLE 8.2

QUESTION: Are you in favor of the death penalty for a person convicted of murder?

	Favor	Oppose	Depends (vol.)	No opinion	Number of interviews
National	77%	13%	8%	2%	1000
Sex					
Male	80	12	6	2	489
Female	74	15	9	2	511
Age					
18-29 years	80	14	4	2	220
30-49 years	77	13	8	2	438
50-64 years	79	12	7	2	175
65 & older	71	13	14	2	159
Region					
East	75	17	8	•	232
Midwest	78	10	9	3	259
South	77	12	8	3	293
West	78	15	6	1	216
Community					
Urban	72	17	8	3	461
Suburban	83	9	7	1	324
Rural	79	11	8	2	213
Race					
White	81	10	7	2	846
Non-white	56	30	12	2	154
Education					
College postgraduate	69	22	7	2	175
College graduate	75	17	6	2	329
Some college	81	9	8	2	281
No college	76	14	8	2	386
Politics					
Republicans	89	7	4	•	284
Democrats	67	20	10	3	286
Independents	76	13	9	2	430
Clinton approval					
Approve	72	16	10	2	499
Disapprove	84	11	5	•	435
Income					
$75,000 & over	78	19	2	1	137
$50,000 & over	81	14	4	1	319
$30,000-49,999	82	7	9	2	213
$20,000-29,999	75	14	8	3	165
Under $20,000	71	17	11	1	252
Importance of religion					
Very	75	13	10	2	537
Fairly	84	10	5	1	312
Not very	69	21	7	3	145
Gun owner					
Yes	84	8	6	2	352

Death Penalty for Murder – Trend

	Favor	Oppose	Depends (vol.)/ no opinion
1995 May 11-14	77%	13%	10%
1994 Sep 6-7	80	16	4
1991 Jun 13-16	76	18	6
1988 Sep 25-Oct 1	79	16	5
1988 Sep 9-11	79	16	5
1985 Nov 11-18	75	17	8
1985 Jan 11-14	72	20	8
1981 Jan 30-Feb 2	66	25	9
1978 Mar 3-6	62	27	11
1976 Apr 9-12	66	26	8
1972 Nov 10-13	57	32	11
1972 Mar 3-5	50	41	9
1971 Oct 29-Nov 2	49	40	11
1969 Jan 23-28	51	40	9
1967 Jun 2-7	54	38	8
1966 May 19-24	42	47	11
1965 Jan 7-12	45	43	12
1960 Mar 2-7	53	36	11
1957 Aug 29-Sep 4	47	34	18
1956 Mar 29-Apr 3	53	34	13
1953 Nov 1-5	68	25	7

• Less than one percent

Source: The Gallup Poll, 1995

was 42 percent (47 percent opposed) in 1966, a period of civil rights and anti-Vietnam War marches, "flower children," and the peace movement. It was also the only time in the 55 years of Gallup polling that those who opposed capital punishment outnumbered those who favored it. As shown in Table 8.2, those least likely to favor the death penalty were women, Democrats, urban dwellers, older people, and nonWhites. Nonetheless, a majority of each demographic group still favored the death penalty.

College freshmen hold similar views as the general public toward capital punishment. The Higher Education Research Institute survey has found that a growing proportion of freshmen favor the death penalty. While over half the freshmen surveyed in 1969 opposed capital punishment, only 20.1 percent did so in 1994. As in the population as a whole, over three-quarters of the freshmen surveyed favored the death penalty.

DEATH PENALTY FAVORED EVEN IF SOME ARE INNOCENT

Eight of 10 Americans think that in the past 20 years some innocent people have been sentenced to death. In 1995, even if the experts' estimate of 1 of every 100 people convicted of murder were innocent was correct, three-fourths of those who favored capital punishment still said they would have supported the death penalty. A majority of all Americans (57 percent) continued to favor the death sentence even if mistakes occurred; 15 percent favored it, but not if mistakes occurred; and 4 percent were unsure that mistakes occurred but favored capital punishment anyway. The percent of people who had no opinion on capital punishment rose from 2 percent to 11 percent. (See Table 8.3.)

UNFAIRLY APPLIED

Despite the overwhelming support for the death penalty shown by the American people, many thought that it had been unfairly applied — that the poor and Blacks were more likely to be sentenced to death for murder than those of average or above average income, or Whites. In 1991 (latest poll), 6 in 10 Americans thought that

---

TABLE 8.3

How often do you think a person has been sentenced to the death penalty who was, in fact, innocent of the crime he was charged with? Do you think this has ever happened in the past 20 years, or do you think it has never happened?

Yes, happened in past 20 years	82%
No, never happened	14
No opinion	4
	100%

(Asked of those who favor death penalty, 769 respondents, ±4%) Some experts estimate that one out of a hundred people who have been sentenced to death were actually innocent. If that estimate were right, would you still support the death penalty for a person convicted of a murder, or not?

Yes	74%
No	20
Depends (vol.)	4
No opinion	2
	100%

Summary

Favor, even if mistakes occur	57%
Favor, but not if mistakes occur	15
Favor, unsure if mistakes occur	4
Do not favor	13
No opinion	11
	100%

Source: The Gallup Poll, 1995

TABLE 8.4

QUESTION: As I read off each of these statements would you tell me if you agree or disagree with it (Rotated): (a) A black person is more likely than a white person to receive the death penalty for the same crime; (b) A poor person is more likely than a person of average or above average income to receive the death penalty for the same crime.

| | Blacks | | | Poor people | | | |
	Agree	Dis-agree	No opinion	Agree	Dis agree	No opinion	No of interviews
National	45%	50%	5%	60%	36%	4%	990
Sex							
Male	6	47	7	64	32	4	477
Female	44	52	4	57	39	4	513
Age							
18-29 years	41	55	4	54	44	2	245
30-49 years	50	46	4	67	31	2	377
50 & older	43	50	7	57	35	8	357
Region							
East	45	51	4	59	39	2	254
Midwest	45	47	8	62	33	5	243
South	40	55	5	58	35	7	337
West	52	44	4	64	35	1	156
Race							
White	41	54	5	59	37	4	650
Black	73	20	7	72	22	6	303
Education							
College grads.	54	40	6	70	28	2	241
College inc.	49	48	3	70	29	1	211
High school grads.	41	54	5	55	42	3	397
Not H.S. grads.	39	53	8	47	41	12	136
Politics							
Republicans	33	63	4	54	43	3	280
Democrats	52	42	6	64	30	6	359
Independents	52	44	4	64	34	2	316
Ideology							
Liberal	49	48	3	61	36	3	365
Moderate	57	35	8	85	14	1	68
Conservative	41	55	4	58	40	2	394
Income							
$50,000 & over	49	48	3	65	34	1	165
$30,000-49,999	39	55	6	58	40	2	238
$20,000-29,999	56	40	4	71	27	2	188
Under $20,000	42	51	7	56	36	8	317
Religion							
Protestant	44	51	5	59	36	5	582
Catholic	46	50	4	60	40	•	216
None	47	43	10	69	26	5	80

• Less than one percent

Penalty Unfairly Applied — Trend

	1985	1991
To blacks		
Agree	39%	45%
Disagree	53	50
No opinion	8	5
	100%	100%
To poor people		
Agree	64%	60%
Disagree	31	36
No opinion	5	4
	100%	100%

Source: The Gallup Poll, 1991

TABLE 8.5

Do you think you would, or would not, be able to afford a lawyer to defend you if you were charged with murder?

Would	36%
Would not	62
No opinion	2
	100%

Source: The Gallup Poll, 1995

TABLE 8.6

QUESTION: What do you think should be the penalty for murder — the death penalty or life imprisonment with absolutely no possibility of parole?

Death vs. Life Imprisonment — Trend

	1985	1986	1991
Death penalty	56%	55%	53%
Life in prison	34	35	35
Neither (vol.)	4	4	3
No opinion	6	6	9
	100%	100%	100%

	Death	Life w/o parole	Neither (vol.)	No opinion	No. of interviews
National	53%	35%	3%	9%	990
Sex					
Male	59	30	3	8	477
Female	48	40	3	9	513
Age					
18-29 years	54	39	2	5	245
30-49 years	54	34	4	8	377
50 & older	53	33	2	12	357
Region					
East	53	36	3	8	254
Midwest	50	37	2	11	243
South	53	35	3	9	337
West	58	32	3	7	156
Race					
White	56	32	3	9	650
Black	26	62	2	10	303
Education					
College grads.	50	32	6	12	241
College inc.	59	30	4	7	211
High school grads.	59	33	1	7	397
Not H.S. grads.	36	50	2	12	136
Politics					
Republicans	62	28	3	7	280
Democrats	42	46	4	8	359
Independents	56	33	2	9	316
Ideology					
Liberal	54	37	3	6	365
Moderate	44	39	6	11	68
Conservative	58	33	2	7	394
Income					
$50,000 & over	54	33	4	9	165
$30,000-49,999	56	32	3	9	238
$20,000-29,999	66	27	2	5	188
Under $20,000	46	43	2	9	317
Religion					
Protestant	53	36	3	8	582
Catholic	52	37	2	9	216
None	63	23	6	8	80

Source: The Gallup Poll, 1991

TABLE 8.7

Suppose new evidence showed that the death penalty does *not* act as a deterrent to murder, that is does not lower the murder rate. Would you favor or oppose the death penalty? (Asked only of those who favor the death penalty.)

	1985	1986	1991	1991 Whites	1991 Blacks
Favor	71%	73%	69%	71%	58%
Oppose	21	19	26	24	38
No opinion	8	8	5	5	4
	100%	100%	100%	100%	100%

TABLE 8.8

Suppose new evidence showed that the death penalty acts as a deterrent to murder, that it lowers the murder rate. Would you favor or oppose the death penalty? (Asked only of those who oppose the death penalty.)

	1985	1986	1991	1991 Whites	1991 Blacks
Favor	18%	18%	25%	27%	14%
Oppose	67	71	65	62	81
No opinion	15	11	10	11	5
	100%	100%	100%	100%	100%

FIGURE 8.2

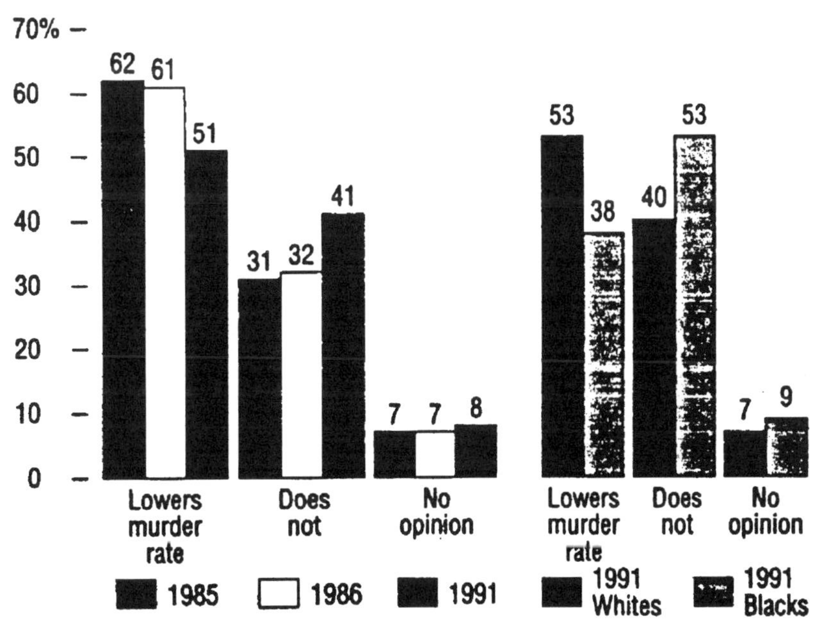

Source of both tables and figure: The Gallup Poll, 1991

the poor were more likely to be given the death penalty than those with higher incomes. Blacks were dramatically more likely to agree than disagree — 72 percent to 22 percent, compared to 59 percent and 37 percent among Whites. (See Table 8.4.)

There was less division among the general public on whether Blacks are more likely to be sentenced to death than Whites. Forty-five percent agreed and 50 percent disagreed, up slightly from the 39 percent who agreed in 1986. As with other aspects of capital punishment, Blacks and Whites often hold opposing views. Almost three-quarters (73 percent) of Blacks believe that Blacks are more likely to be given the death penalty than Whites, compared with 41 percent of Whites.

TABLE 8.9

Why do you favor the death penalty for persons convicted of murder? (Asked only of those who favor, 700 respondents.)

	1985	1991	1991 Whites (500)	1991 Blacks (173)
A life for a life	50%	50%	50%	48%
It is a deterrent	22	13	13	16
Keeps them from killing again	16	19	18	23
Costly to keep them in prison	10	13	14	2
Judicial system is too lenient	3	3	3	2
Other	9	11	10	16
No opinion	2	2	2	2

Note: totals add to more than 100% due to multiple responses

TABLE 8.10

Why do you oppose the death penalty for persons convicted of murder? (Asked only of those who oppose, 217 respondents.)

	1985	1991	1991 Whites (111)	1991 Blacks (99)
Wrong to take a life	40%	41%	40%	44%
Punishment should be left to God	15	17	17	20
Persons may be wrongly convicted	15	11	10	16
Does not deter	5	7	8	7
Possibility of rehabilitation	5	6	6	4
Unfair application of penalty	3	6	5	5
Other	7	16	18	8
No opinion	16	6	6	7

Note: Totals add to more than 100% due to multiple answers

Source of both tables: The Gallup Poll, 1991

AFFORDING A LAWYER

In 1995, most Americans believed that they would not be able to afford a lawyer to defend themselves if they were charged with murder (Table 8.5). This opinion came at a time when most people were watching O. J. Simpson's trial. They were certainly aware of the high cost of his lawyers and for other high profile cases such as the Mendendez Brothers' first trial.

LIFE WITHOUT PAROLE

Support for the death penalty would decline substantially from 76 percent to 53 percent if life in prison with no possibility of parole were certain (1991 poll). (See Table 8.2 and 8.6.) Among Whites, the proportion favoring the death penalty would drop from 78 percent to 56 percent; among Blacks, it would decease from 59 percent to 26 percent.

DETERRENT OR NOT?

Views on the death penalty appear to be very well entrenched. In 1991, the Gallup Poll asked those who supported the death penalty whether they would continue to support it if new evidence were found that it neither acted as a deterrent nor lowered the murder rate, and asked those who opposed the death penalty if they would continue to oppose it if it were determined that it did act as a deterrent to murder and did lower the murder rate. By very similar percentages, only about 1 in 4 of both those favoring and opposing capital punishment indicated that new evidence would change their minds (Tables 8.7 and 8.8).

TABLE 8.11

QUESTION: When a teenager commits a murder and is found guilty by a jury, do you think he should get the death penalty or shold be spared because of his youth?

For teenagers?

	Favor	Oppose	No opinion	No. of interviews
National	60%	30%	10%	1022
Sex				
Male	66	26	8	523
Female	56	33	11	499
Age				
18-29 years	60	30	10	192
30-49 years	62	30	8	458
50-64 years	55	34	11	193
65 & older	63	25	12	174
Region				
East	57	32	11	261
Midwest	59	31	10	262
South	64	28	8	288
West	60	29	11	211
Community				
Urban	60	31	9	403
Suburban	61	30	9	345
Rural	60	28	12	266
Race				
White	60	30	10	891
Non-white	59	33	8	114
Education				
College postgrad.	52	39	9	150
College graduate	59	33	8	313
Some college	59	27	14	282
No college	63	29	8	425
Politics				
Republicans	65	24	11	347
Democrats	56	37	7	300
Independents	61	28	11	375
Ideology				
Liberal	53	35	12	183
Moderate	61	30	9	395
Conservative	63	28	9	418
Clinton approval				
Approve	54	36	10	392
Disapprove	65	26	9	567
Income				
$75.000 & over	68	28	4	115
$50.000 & over	62	30	8	278
$30.000-49,999	60	31	9	284
$20.000-29,999	66	22	12	173
Under $20,000	55	33	12	228

Source: The Gallup Poll, 1994

Interestingly, only a bare majority (51 percent) of Americans considered the death penalty a deterrent to murder or that it lowered the murder rate; 41 percent believed that it did not lower the murder rate (Figure 8.2).

Reasons For and Against Capital Punishment

In 1991, when the Gallup Poll asked those who favored capital punishment why they supported it, the largest proportion (50 percent) indicated revenge, followed by the belief that it kept the killers from killing again (19 percent), it was too costly to keep them in prison (13 percent), and that it acted as a deterrent (13 percent) (Table 8.9). Those opposing capital punishment overwhelmingly cited their belief that it was wrong to take a life (41 percent), followed by a belief that punishment should be left to God (17 percent), and fear of wrongful convictions (11 percent) (Table 8.10).

DEATH PENALTY FOR JUVENILES

As Americans become more concerned about crime, they tend to favor tougher penalties. In 1957, only 11 percent of those polled favored the death penalty for teenagers who committed murders and were found guilty by a jury. By 1994, 6 of 10 of those polled agreed. Women, those 50 to 64 years old, Easterners, those with a postgraduate college education, Democrats, and those with incomes under $20,000 were the least likely to favor capital punishment for juveniles. (See Table 8.11.) Of those who supported the death penalty for adults, one-quarter (24 percent) favored capital punishment for juveniles in 1957. By 1994, almost three-fourths (72 percent) supported it (Table 8.12).

MOST HUMANE FORM OF EXECUTION

The Gallup Poll (1991) found that a majority of people (66 percent) thought lethal injection was the most humane form of execution followed at a great distance by the electric chair (10 percent) and the gas chamber (6 percent). Not many rated the firing squad (3 percent) or hanging (3 percent) as most humane. (See Table 8.13.)

EUROPEAN ATTITUDES

The increased number of executions in 1995 and 1996, including one by firing squad and one by hanging, has intensified the belief of many Europeans that America is a "savage" country with medieval views. In response, European legislatures and human-right groups stepped up their campaigns against capital punishment in the United States. Many European leaders see the abolition of the capital punishment as a sign of a mature society and require countries admitted to the Council of Europe to abolish the death penalty. For example, Poland had to agree to abolish capital punishment upon joining.

Gino Concetti, a columnist with the Vatican daily *L'Ossevatore Romano*, commented that "European citizens have already made their choice, they have abolished the death penalty [except for some countries in the former Soviet bloc], and I deplore the fact that in a democratic country like the United States the death penalty is still used. A Swedish legislator, Hanna Zetterberg, is leading a letter-writing campaign to prevent more executions in the United States. The Swedish Medical Association and the Swedish Psychological Association have written U.S. politicians, asking for clemency for death-row inmates. The U.S. Embassy in Bonn receives about 150 letters each month from Germans protesting the death penalty.

CHAPTER IX

CAPITAL PUNISHMENT AROUND THE WORLD

Capital punishment is not only controversial in the United States, but in many other countries of the world. The ethical arguments which fuel the debate in the United States also characterize the discussion in other countries. The United Nations' position on capital punishment is a product of compromise among those nations which want it completely abolished, those which want it maintained for serious offenses, and those which believe the issue should be left to each nation to decide. In 1957, after 11 years of debate, a compromise statement on the death penalty was included in the International Covenant on Civil and Political Rights, which the General Assembly adopted in its Resolution 2200 (XXI) of December 16, 1966. Article 6 of the Covenant reads,

1. Every human being has the inherent right to life. This right shall be protected by law. No one shall be arbitrarily deprived of his life.

2. In countries which have not abolished the death penalty, sentence of death may be imposed only for the most serious crimes in accordance with the law in force at the time of the commission of the crime and not contrary to the provisions of the present Covenant and to the Convention on the Prevention and Punishment of the Crime of Genocide. This penalty can only be carried out pursuant to a final judgment rendered by a competent court.

3. When deprivation of life constitutes the crime of genocide, it is understood that nothing in this article shall authorize any State Party to the present Covenant to derogate in any way from any obligation assumed under the provisions of the Convention on the Prevention and Punishment of the Crime of Genocide.

4. Anyone sentenced to death shall have the right to seek pardon or commutation of the sentence. Amnesty, pardon, or commutation of the sentence of death may be granted in all cases.

5. Sentence of death shall not be imposed for crimes committed by persons below eighteen years of age and shall not be carried out on pregnant women.

6. Nothing in this article shall be invoked to delay or prevent the abolition of capital punishment by any State Party to the present Covenant.

The United Nations has dealt with the death penalty in several other documents and meetings. Among them is General Assembly Resolution 2393 (XXIII) of November 26, 1968, which specifies legal safeguards that every country using capital punishment should offer condemned prisoners, namely:

(i) A person condemned to death shall not be deprived of the right to appeal to a higher judicial authority or, as the case may be, to petition for pardon or reprieve;

(ii) A death sentence shall not be carried out until the procedures of appeal or, as the case may be, of petition for pardon or reprieve have been terminated;

(iii) Special attention be given in the case of indigent persons by the provision of adequate legal assistance at all stages of the proceedings.

General Assembly Resolution 2857 (XXVI) of December 20, 1971 observed,

TABLE 9.1

<u>RETENTIONIST</u>

*(Countries which retain and use the death penalty for ordinary crimes)**

<u>Country</u>

AFGHANISTAN	INDONESIA	SAINT CHRISTOPHER AND
ALGERIA	IRAN	NEVIS
ANTIGUA AND BARBUDA	IRAQ	SAINT LUCIA
ARMENIA	JAMAICA	SAINT VINCENT AND THE
AZERBAYDZHAN	JAPAN	GRENADINES
BAHAMAS	JORDAN	SAUDI ARABIA
BANGLADESH	KAZAKHSTAN	SIERRA LEONE
BARBADOS	KENYA	SINGAPORE
BELARUS	KOREA (Democratic	SOMALIA
BELIZE	People's Republic) North Korea]	SUDAN
BENIN	KOREA (Republic)	SWAZILAND
BOSNIA-HERZEGOVINA	[South Korea]	SYRIA
BOTSWANA	KUWAIT	TADZHIKISTAN
BULGARIA	KYRGYZSTAN	TAIWAN (Republic of
BURKINA FASO	LAOS	China)
CAMEROON	LATVIA	TANZANIA
CHAD	LEBANON	THAILAND
CHILE	LESOTHO	TRINIDAD AND TOBAGO
CHINA (People's Republic)	LIBERIA	TUNISIA
CUBA	LIBYA	TURKMENISTAN
DOMINICA	LITHUANIA	UGANDA
EGYPT	MALAWI	UKRAINE
EQUATORIAL GUINEA	MALAYSIA	UNITED ARAB EMIRATES
ERITREA	MAURITANIA	UNITED STATES OF
ESTONIA	MAURITIUS	AMERICA
ETHIOPIA	MONGOLIA	UZBEKISTAN
GABON	MOROCCO	VIET NAM
GEORGIA	MYANMAR	YEMEN
GHANA	NIGERIA	YUGOSLAVIA (Federal
GRENADA	OMAN	Republic of)
GUATEMALA	PAKISTAN	ZAIRE
GUINEA	POLAND QATAR	ZAMBIA
GUYANA	RUSSIA	ZIMBABWE
INDIA		

<u>TOTAL: 94 countries and territories</u>

---

* Most of these countries and territories are known to have carried out executions during the past 10 years. On some countries Amnesty International has no record of executions but is unable to ascertain whether or not executions have in fact been carried out. Several countries have carried out executions in the past 10 years but have since instituted national moratoria on executions.

Source: *The Death Penalty: List of Abolitionist and Retentionist Countries (September 1995)*, AI Index: ACT 50/06/95, Amnesty International, London, United Kingdom, 1995

TABLE 9.2

<u>ABOLITIONIST DE FACTO</u>

(Countries and territories which retain the death penalty for ordinary crimes but can be considered abolitionist in practice in that they have not executed anyone during the past 10 years or more, or in that they have made an international commitment not to carry out executions)

<u>Country</u>	<u>Date of Last Execution</u>
ALBANIA*	
BAHRAIN	1977
BELGIUM	1950
BERMUDA	1977
BHUTAN	1964**
BOLIVIA	1974
BRUNEI DARUSSALAM	1957
BURUNDI	1982
CENTRAL AFRICAN REPUBLIC	1981
CONGO	1982
COMOROS	***
COTE D'IVOIRE	
DJIBOUTI	***
GAMBIA	1981
MADAGASCAR	1958**
MALDIVES	1952**
MALI	1980
MOLDOVA****	1989
NAURU	***
NIGER	1976**
PAPUA NEW GUINEA	1950
PHILIPPINES	1976
RWANDA	1982
SENEGAL	1967
SRI LANKA	1976
SURINAME	1982
TOGO	
TONGA	1982
TURKEY	1984
WESTERN SAMOA	***

<u>TOTAL: 30 countries and territories</u>

---

*   Preparatory to Albania's joining the Council of Europe, in a declaration signed on 29 June, Pjeter Arbnori, President of the Albanian Parliament, said he was willing to commit his country "to put into place a moratorium on executions until [the] total abolition of capital punishment".

**   Date of last known execution

***   No executions since independence

****   Preparatory to joining the Council of Europe, Moldova committed itself on 27 June "to uphold the moratorium on executions until the total abolition of capital punishment".

Source: *The Death Penalty: List of Abolitionist and Retentionist Countries (September 1995)*,
AI Index: ACT 50/06/95, Amnesty International, London, United Kingdom, 1995

In order to guarantee fully the right to life, provided for in Article 3 of the Universal Declaration of Human Rights, the main objective to be pursued is that of progressively restricting the number of offenses for which capital punishment may be imposed, with a view to the desirability of abolishing this punishment in all countries.

The Economic and Social Council Resolution 1574(L) of the same year made a similar declaration. According to the Report of the Secretary-General on Capital Punishment (February 8, 1980),

The United Nations has gradually shifted from the position of a neutral observer concerned about, but not committed, on the question of the death penalty, to a position favoring the eventual abolition of the death penalty. From the moral standpoint, the United Nations has followed the guidance of the Universal Declaration of Human Rights. From the practical or utilitarian point of view, [the United Nations has] called only for the "eventual abolition of capital punishment."

RETENTIONIST COUNTRIES

Amnesty International, a human rights organization headquartered in London, England, maintains information on capital punishment throughout the world. (Amnesty International vehemently opposes the death penalty, considering it the "ultimate form of cruel, inhuman, and degrading punishment.") The organization refers to countries which retain and use the death penalty as retentionist; those who no longer use the death penalty are known as abolitionist.

As of fall, 1995, less than half the nations and territories in the world (94 countries, down from 103 countries in 1993) used the death penalty as a possible punishment for ordinary crimes* (Table 9.1), although some had not carried out an execution in many years.

The death penalty has become increasingly rare among the Western industrially developed countries. Only Belgium (which maintains the death penalty on the books, but has not executed anyone in more than 40 years — *de facto* abolitionist, see below) and the United States (the federal government and 38 states) still permit capital punishment.

In November 1995, many countries condemned Nigeria for hanging Ken Saro-Wiwa, one of the country's leading environmentalists and authors, and eight other human rights activists. Protesters of the execution claimed that the men were framed for the murders of four pro-military leaders. The U.S. Great Britain, and several other countries withdrew their ambassadors, the Commonwealth suspended Nigeria from its membership, the European Union pulled its representative from the country, and the World Bank rejected a $100 million loan to Nigeria.

DE FACTO ABOLITIONISTS

Thirty countries and territories, up from 19 countries in 1993, have not executed a prisoner for at least the past decade, although the death penalty is still formally part of their law (Table 9.2). Amnesty International considers these nations, some of which have not executed anyone for the past 30 years or more, to have abolished capital punishment on a *de facto* basis — in practice if not in law.

---

*"Ordinary" crimes such as murder, rape, and, in some countries, robbery or embezzlement of very large amounts of money are those committed during the normal course of a community's activities. "Exceptional" crimes are those committed in the military or in extraordinary times, most notably during a war, such as treason, spying, or desertion.

TABLE 9.3

ABOLITIONIST FOR ALL CRIMES
(Countries and territories whose laws do not provide for the death penalty for any crime)

Country	Date of Abolition	Date of Abolition for Ordinary Crimes	Date of Last Execution
ANDORRA	1990		1943
ANGOLA	1992		
AUSTRALIA	1985	1984	1967
AUSTRIA	1968	1950	1950
CAMBODIA	1989		
CAPE VERDE	1981		1835
COLOMBIA	1910		1909
COSTA RICA	1877		
CROATIA	1990		
CZECH REPUBLIC	1990*		
DENMARK	1978	1933	1950
DOMINICAN REPUBLIC	1966		
ECUADOR	1906		
FINLAND	1972	1949	1944
FRANCE	1981		1977
GERMANY	1949/1987**		1949**
GREECE	1993		1972
GUINEA-BISSAU	1993		1986***
HAITI	1987		1972***
HONDURAS	1956		1940
HONG KONG	1993		1966
HUNGARY	1990		1988
ICELAND	1928		1830
IRELAND	1990		1954
ITALY	1994	1947	1947
KIRIBATI			****
LIECHTENSTEIN	1987		1785
LUXEMBOURG	1979		1949
MACEDONIA			
MARSHALL ISLANDS			****
MICRONESIA (Federated States)			****
MONACO	1962		1847
MOZAMBIQUE	1990		1986
NAMIBIA	1990		1988***
NETHERLANDS	1982	1870	1952
NEW ZEALAND	1989	1961	1957
NICARAGUA	1979		1930
NORWAY	1979	1905	1948
PALAU			
PANAMA			1903***
PORTUGAL	1976	1867	1849***
ROMANIA	1989		1989
SAN MARINO	1865	1848	1468***
SAO TOME AND PRINCIPE	1990		****
SLOVAK REPUBLIC	1990*		
SLOVENIA	1989		
SOLOMON ISLANDS		1966	****
SWEDEN	1972	1921	1910
SWITZERLAND	1992	1942	1944
TUVALU			****
URUGUAY	1907		
VANUATU			****
VATICAN CITY STATE	1969		
VENEZUELA	1863		

TOTAL: 54 countries

* The death penalty was abolished in the Czech and Slovak Federal Republic in 1990. On 1 January 1993 the Czech and Slovak Federal Republic divided into two states, the Czech Republic and the Slovak Republic. The last execution in the Czech and Slovak Federal Republic was in 1988.

** The death penalty was abolished in the Federal Republic of Germany (FRG) in 1949 and in the German Democratic Republic (GDR) in 1987. The last execution in the FRG was in 1949; the date of the last execution in the GDR is not known. The FRG and the GDR were unified in October 1990.

*** Date of last known execution

**** No executions since independence

Source: *The Death Penalty: List of Abolitionist and Retentionist Countries (September 1995)*, AI
Index: ACT 50/06/95, Amnesty International, London, United Kingdom, 1995

ABOLITIONIST NATIONS

In 1863, Venezuela became the first nation to institute an effective abolitionist regulation on the death penalty. Since that time, many nations have abolished capital punishment, although many countries, such as Argentina, Brazil, Nepal, and Spain, restored it after previously rejecting it. Argentina abolished the death penalty for all crimes in 1921 and 1972, but reinstated it in 1976, only to abolish it again in 1984. Brazil abolished the death penalty in 1882, restored it in 1969, and abolished it again in 1979. Similarly, Spain abolished it in 1932, returned it for certain crimes in 1934, totally restored it in 1938, and then abolished it again in 1978. This succession of abolition and restoration often reflects a nation's fluctuation between democratic and authoritarian forms of governments.

As of September 1995, 54 countries had abolished the death penalty for all crimes (Table 9.3). Amnesty International reported that during 1992 and 1993, five countries — Angola, Switzerland, Guinea-Bissau, Greece, and Hong Kong — abolished the death penalty for all crimes. In 1994, Italy abolished the death penalty for all crimes. Abolition by the Czech and Slovak Federal Republic in 1990 (they became two independent republics in 1993), following a

---

TABLE 9.4

ABOLITIONIST FOR ORDINARY CRIMES ONLY

(Countries whose laws provide for the death penalty only for exceptional crimes such as crimes under military law or crimes committed in exceptional circumstances such as wartime)

Country	Date of Abolition	Date of Last Execution
ARGENTINA	1984	
BRAZIL	1979	1855
CANADA	1976	1962
CYPRUS	1983	1962
EL SALVADOR	1983	1973*
FIJI	1979	1964
ISRAEL	1954	1962
MALTA	1971	1943
MEXICO		1937
NEPAL	1990	1979
PARAGUAY	1992	1928
PERU	1979	1979
SEYCHELLES		**
SOUTH AFRICA	1995	1991
SPAIN	1978	1975
UNITED KINGDOM	1973	1964

TOTAL: 16 countries

---

* Date of last known execution
** No executions since independence

Source: *The Death Penalty: List of Abolitionist and Retentionist Countries (September 1995)*, AI Index: ACT 50/06/95, Amnesty International, London, United Kingdom, 1995

similar move by Hungary in 1989 and the German Democratic Republic in 1987, indicated the sweeping political changes then taking place in Eastern Europe. In 1990, the German Democratic Republic became part of the Federal Republic of Germany, which had abolished the death penalty in 1949, following World War II. Slovenia and Croatia stopped the death penalty while they were still part of Yugoslavia. In 1991, they became independent countries.

Abolitionist Countries for "Ordinary Crimes"

Sixteen countries do not have the death penalty for "ordinary" crimes (Table 9.4). Recently, Nepal (1990), Paraguay (1992), and South Africa (1995) eliminated the death penalty for ordinary crimes. On June 6, 1995, the South African Supreme Court abolished the death penalty, stating that "everyone, including the most abominable of human beings, has a right to life, and capital punishment is therefore unconstitutional." The court continued, "Retribution cannot be accorded the same weight under our Constitution as the right to life and dignity. It has to be shown that the death sentence would be materially more effective to deter or prevent murder than the alternative sentence of life imprisonment would be."

Prior to the court's ruling, the government had stopped executing prisoners in 1992, often because the death sentence was not used as punishments for crimes but as a means to enforce the political system of apartheid. With violent crime increasing in the 1990s, the number of people on death row numbered 443. These prisoners would now be removed from death row. In the 1980s more than 1,100 people had been executed by hanging in South Africa.

The country is divided about the decision, especially along racial lines. While Whites expressed their fear of crime spreading without severe enough punishment, Blacks noted that in the past they had often been victims of the death penalty through wrongful arrests and convictions. Because the death penalty had been applied more to Blacks than Whites under apartheid, it has become an emotional issue. The African National Congress stated that "never, never, and never again must citizens of our country be subjected to the barbaric practice of capital punishment." Archbishop Tutu, the Anglican primate of Southern Africa, told the South African Press Association that "it's making us a civilized nation. It shows we actually do mean business when we say we have reverence for life." Conservative White groups retorted that "the rights of murderers and rapists are being held in a higher regard than those of their victims."

JAPAN

The Japanese have become very focused on the death penalty since the arrest of 30 members of the religious cult Aum Shinri Kyo in connection with the nerve gas attack in the subways. Since World War II, almost 600 people have been executed, 7 in 1993, although there were no executions in the three preceding years. The legal process to carry out an execution can be very drawn-out. One man has been under sentence of death for 27 years, and two for 26 years.

Many Asian observers believe their cultures have a different attitude towards capital punishment than most Western cultures. In a *New York Times* interview, Tadashi Utematshu, a law professor, commented, "In Japan it's important to be seen as punishing people who have done wrong. Maybe Japan has a greater sense of justice, while Europe has greater respect for human life." Similarly, a Taiwan official said, "We in Asia are more concerned with justice and punishment. You in the West have a Christian tradition that emphasizes mercy, and so you are more reluctant to execute people. You always want to forgive people."

CHAPTER X

THE DEBATE — CAPITAL PUNISHMENT SHOULD BE MAINTAINED

PREPARED STATEMENT OF REPRESEN-TATIVE ROBERT K. DORNAN (R-CA), DECEMBER 4, 1995.

As a U.S. congressman, one of my primary concerns is the rule of law. Over the last thirty years, our nation has experienced a crippling decline in effective law enforcement resulting from the erosion of the concept of swift and sure punishment for law breakers. This has resulted from multiple causes, including a politicized judiciary, which all too often has been more sympathetic to the criminal than the victim, and as well, to a general judicial philosophy which has become more concerned with questions of procedure than the search for truth....

As a conservative, I believe there are certain crimes for which the death penalty is justified. Some individuals commit crimes so reprehensible that they forfeit their right to live in society. And some commit crimes so heinous that they do not deserve to be supported for life by the society they injured. These are the people who should be sentenced to death. The death penalty should remain our most severe punishment, and should be used only in extraordinary cases. But as has always been the standard in our justice system, the punishment should fit the crime.

PREPARED STATEMENT OF REPRESEN-TATIVE SAM JOHNSON (R-TX), NOVEM-BER 8, 1995.

Regarding capital punishment, I continue to believe that the best way to prevent crime is to target repeat offenders. Criminals must understand the consequences of their actions. We should make prisoners serve out their entire sentences and enforce stiffer penalties such as capital punishment against felons convicted of heinous crimes such as rape, murder, and drug-related deaths. I am aware of the need for individual responsibility in determining the death penalty's applicability, and we must always be diligent not to punish the innocent. However, in spite of these risks, I believe that capital punishment is a morally justifiable, necessary, and effective punishment.

Thirty-six states currently administer capital punishment. Texas alone has executed 99 criminals in the past 7 years. The people of Texas have made it known that violent crime will not be tolerated.

PREPARED STATEMENT OF SENATOR JESSE HELMS (R-SC), NOVEMBER 6, 1995.

Although I wish that the death penalty was never necessary, I do believe that it should be available to our courts to punish those responsible for especially violent crimes. I believe that the death penalty protects society from further harm by the offender. I also think that it is useful in deterring others from committing similar crimes.

American society will be increasingly plagued by violent crime without the use of the death penalty. In order to combat crime, we must give our police officers and judges the support and encouragement necessary to get tough with

99

criminals. The death penalty is one step in the <u>right</u> direction.

EXCERPTS FROM JUSTICE ANTONIN SCALIA'S OPINION CONCURRING IN THE SUPREME COURT'S ORDER DENYING REVIEW IN A TEXAS DEATH PENALTY CASE, FEBRUARY 22, 1994. (THIS WAS IN RESPONSE TO JUSTICE BLACKMUN'S DISSENT. SEE CHAPTER XI.)

The Fifth Amendment provides that "[n]o persons shall be held to answer for a capital crime, unless on a presentment or indictment of a Grand Jury, nor be deprived of life without due process of law." This clearly permits the death penalty to be imposed, and establishes beyond doubt that the death penalty is not one of the "cruel and unusual punishments" prohibited by the Eighth Amendment....

Convictions in opposition to the death penalty are often passionate and deeply held. That would be no excuse for reading them into a Constitution that does not contain them, even if they represented the convictions of a majority of Americans. Much less is there any excuse for using that course to thrust a minority's views upon the people....

If people conclude ... that brutal deaths may be deterred by capital punishment; indeed, if they merely conclude that justice requires such brutal deaths to be avenged by capital punishment; the creation of false, untextual and unhistorical contradictions within the "Court's Eighth Amendment jurisprudence" shall not prevent them.

STATEMENT OF PAUL G. CASSELL, ASSOCIATE PROFESSOR OF LAW, UNIVERSITY OF UTAH, SALT LAKE CITY, BEFORE THE SENATE JUDICIARY COMMITTEE, APRIL 1, 1993.

The paucity of examples of innocent defendants who have been executed provides compelling evidence that the risk of mistaken execution is virtually non-existent. If opponents of the death penalty are able to produce no better examples of mistaken executions (in the testimony), then the overwhelming majority of Americans who support capital punishment can rest assured that the criminal justice system is doing an admirable, if not indeed perfect, job of preventing the execution of innocent defendants....

Capital sentences, when carried out, save innocent lives by permanently incapacitating murders. Some persons who commit capital homicide will slay other innocent persons if given the opportunity to do so. The death penalty is the most effective means of preventing such killers from repeating their crimes. The next most serious penalty, life imprisonment without possibility of parole, prevents murderers from committing some crimes but does not prevent them from murdering in prison.

At least five Federal prison officers have been killed since December 1982, and the inmates in at least three of the incidents were already serving life sentences for murder....

While the innocent lives saved through the incapacitative effect of capital punishment are important, the penalty also saves far more innocent lives through its general deterrent effect....

Logic supports the conclusion that the death penalty is the most effective deterrent for some kinds of murders — those that require reflection and forethought by persons of reasonable intelligence and unimpaired mental facilities. Many capital offenses are quintessential contemplative offenses. Murder for hire, treason, and terrorist bombings all require extensive planning. It stands to reason that capital punishment deters such persons more than the next most serious penalty, life imprisonment without parole.

Anecdotal evidence in support of the deterrent value of capital sentences comes from examples of persons who have been deterred from murdering, or risking a murder, because of the death penalty. For instance, Justice McComb of the California Supreme Court collected from the files of the Los Angeles Police Department fourteen examples within a four-year period of defendants who, in explaining their refusal to take a life or carry a weapon, pointed to the presence of the death penalty....

Statistical studies support the proposition that capital sentences, like other criminal sanctions, have a deterrent effect. To be sure, some statistical surveys, often conducted by opponents of the death penalty, have found no such effect....

One of the most recent substantial econometric studies was performed by Professor Stephen K. Layson of the University of North Carolina at Greensboro, who analyzed data for the United States from 1936 to 1977. Layson concluded that increases in the probability of execution reduced the homicide rate. Specifically, Layson found that, on average, each execution deterred approximately eighteen murders....

Through the imposition of just punishment, civilized society expressed its outrage and sense of revulsion toward those who, by contravening its laws, have not only inflicted injury upon discrete individuals, but also weakened the bonds that hold communities together. Certain crimes constitute such outrageous violation of human and moral values that they demand retribution. It was to control the natural human impulse to seek revenge and, more broadly, to give expression to deeply held views that some conduct deserves punishment, that criminal laws, administered by the State, were established. The rule of law does not eliminate feelings of outrage but does provide controlled channels for expressing such feelings. People can rely on society to sanction criminal conduct and to carry out deserved punishments....

The death penalty's retributive function thus vindicates the fundamental moral principle that a criminal should receive his or her just desserts. Through the provision of just punishment, capital punishment affirms the sanctity of human life and thereby protects it.

... the system imposes a vast array of due process protections to assure that no innocent person is convicted of a crime.

PREPARED STATEMENT OF MIRIAM SHEHANE, STATE PRESIDENT, VICTIMS OF CRIME AND LENIENCY, MONTGOMERY, ALABAMA, BEFORE THE SENATE JUDICIARY COMMITTEE, APRIL 1, 1993.

My daughter, Quenette, was brutally murdered in 1976....

Time will not permit nor will I burden you with the gory details of how one of the defendants described her hours of torture and final death but the memory is imprinted in my mind permanently. The three men who killed her were arrested and brought to trial — literally 7 trials over a period of 6 years.... The frustrations the families go through when they think justice will soon prevail, only to receive jolt after jolt as they learn the case is going back for trial due to technicalities, is enough to cause fatal health problems.

... As you know, 36 States have determined that the death penalty is the most appropriate punishment for certain brutal and vicious murders. As the parent of a murder victim, I feel this punishment is not only fair, it is essential. What is not fair is when this punishment is prolonged by extensive appeals, stays, and postponements. We victims need a closure to our grief. I did not rejoice when Wallace Norrell was executed July 13, 1990 for murdering Quenette, but I certainly felt relief. I could not have a sense of completion and finally put my dear Quenette to rest if I didn't have to worry about two others being released at some point....

I can assure you that the system as it now operates gives far more consideration to death row inmates than it affords the victim and their families. What are the safeguards for the victim when a murderer is tried, acquitted by a jury, but can never be retried no matter how much evidence is produced in the future? Are the scales of justice earnestly balanced when a convicted murderer is not executed for 13½ years? Lest we forget, in addition to the extensive appeals of the courts, every State with a capital punishment statute has a procedure for executive clemency....

STATEMENT OF JAMES TRAFICANT (D-OH), IN THE *CONGRESSIONAL RECORD*, MAY 25, 1993.

It is time to enact the death penalty for first-degree murder. We have been coddling murderers too long, and we have been, in fact, denying victims any rights or protections. What do we now tell this family in Lansing, MI? That the murderer who killed your father and who had a lifetime sentence will be given another lifetime sentence? This is unbelievable, and nobody in Washington is doing one thing about it. It is time ... to stop reading tombstones all over America and legislate and create some policy on first degree murder.

STATEMENT OF JOHN C. SCULLY, COUNSEL, WASHINGTON LEGAL FOUNDATION, WASHINGTON, DC, BEFORE THE HOUSE JUDICIARY COMMITTEE, MAY 3, 1990.

The overwhelming majority of Americans, black and white, support the death penalty. The Supreme Court has consistently upheld the constitutionality of the death penalty. The drug war killings and the other murders that occur daily in our country demonstrate the need for the death penalty. The death penalty is a deterrent to future murders. Finally, some murders are so shocking that it is evident that there is no other punishment that fits the crime.

Yet the will of the majority of the people is regularly frustrated by the opponents of the death penalty who repeatedly devise new and often bizarre forms of lethal attacks upon the death penalty. The rejection by the U.S. Supreme Court of the statistical disparity death by racial quota theory has led the anti-death penalty advocates to seek a legislative vehicle to attack the death penalty....

WLF [Washington Legal Foundation] strongly opposes racial discrimination in the justice system. Individuals sentenced to death should and do have the right and opportunity to challenge any act of racial discrimination in the justice system.

... The BJS [Bureau of Justice Statistics] report showed that for every 1,000 whites arrested on homicide charges, approximately 16 were given a death sentence, while fewer than 12 blacks were sent to death row for every 1,000 blacks arrested for homicide. This means that white murderers are 36% more likely to be sentenced to death than their black counterparts.

Does that mean that white murderers are the victims of racial discrimination? Of course not. There are numerous individual circumstances that comprise each murder case; those circumstances make it impossible to use statistics to prove discrimination in a manner similar to that utilized in employment discrimination cases.

... Studies, unable to show racial discrimination against blacks by examining the race of the defendant, also examined the race of the victim. The Baldus study concluded that for some types of murders, if the victim of the crime was white, then the murderer was more likely to receive a death sentence than if the victim was black.

The race-of-the-victim theory, if accepted, means that even a white murderer can level charges of racism at a jury that sent him to death row for killing a white person....

The Katz study showed that the black defendant/white victim cases are the most aggravated of the four defendant-victim racial combinations. The interracial nature of this kind of homicide minimized the possibility that the killing arose due to a family dispute or fight between friends, neighbors, or relatives.

The black defendant/black victim homicides occurred most frequently and were characterized by poor defendants who kill family members, friends, or other acquaintances during a fight or argument. Those types of murders generally have the most mitigating circumstances.

The white defendant/white victim homicides reflected a mix between killings precipitated by a dispute similar to those precipitating black-on-black homicides, but with a substantial percent (about one third) of the killings comparable to the black-on-white homicides.

Only 27 of the 1,082 cases were characterized as white defendant/black victim homicides. The relatively small number of such homicides made them difficult for Katz to classify.

TESTIMONY OF CONGRESSMAN MATTHEW J. RINALDO (R-NJ), BEFORE THE HOUSE JUDICIARY COMMITTEE, MAY 9, 1990.

It is well-established that an overwhelming majority of the American people support the death penalty for criminals who commit murder. We have a duty to protect the American people from violent individuals. In certain circumstances, the death penalty is the only appropriate and just punishment. It serves as a deterrent to those who could commit such outrageous crimes. Moreover, the perpetrators of these brutal crimes deserve a punishment which fits the crime.

STATEMENT OF BRUCE FEIN, PRIVATE ATTORNEY SPECIALIZING IN CONSTITUTIONAL AND COMMUNICATIONS LAWS, BEFORE HOUSE JUDICIARY COMMITTEE, MAY 23, 1990.

... although the death penalty certainly is not the answer to the worrisome ... levels of crime today, it is an important tool, I think, in creating a right kind of moral climate that suggests there are certain standards of behavior that must be accepted in order to avoid degeneration of society, anarchy and a level of bestiality....

We must recognize that death laws have tongues. They speak to a moral universe that places some kind of conduct simply beyond the level of decent mankind....

It seems to me as well that certainly when you speak of the need for a death penalty for [killing] prison wardens, that would not threaten somebody who is already in prison under a life term with no possibility of parole, and who has very little incentive to do anything to control his conduct, to try to escape, to kill to escape because there isn't any further punishment that is available if death is not an option.

I think we owe a certain decency toward our prison wardens who undertake very dangerous positions to have that death penalty option there.

Lastly, with regard to the deterrent effect of the death penalty. I don't think the way it is administered at present really gives a fair portrayal of what might be the deterrent effect because the delay in imposition is so prolonged, 7 to 8 years.

If the deterrent is going to be genuine, it has to be in some sense permanent and fixed in the mind of a criminal.

STATEMENT OF JOSEPH L. HOFFMANN, PROFESSOR, INDIANA UNIVERSITY AT BLOOMINGTON SCHOOL OF LAW, BLOOMINGTON, INDIANA, BEFORE THE HOUSE JUDICIAL COMMITTEE, MAY 23, 1990.

I support the use of the death penalty for certain extremely serious crimes. I support it not because I believe it has been shown to have a deterrent effect. The evidence is inconclusive at best and probably suggests that the death penalty does not have a significant deterrent effect, at least not the way we do it today.

I support the death penalty for certain very serious crimes simply because I think that it is consistent with our notion of proportional punishment. I think there are serious crimes for which death is the appropriate punishment.

STATEMENT BY JAMES C. ANDERS, SOLICITOR, FIFTH JUDICIAL CIRCUIT, STATE OF SOUTH CAROLINA, BEFORE THE SENATE JUDICIARY COMMITTEE, SEPTEMBER 19, 1989.

I believe that in certain cases, the death penalty can be shown to be the only rational and realistic punishment for an unspeakable crime.... Obviously, the most basic right a citizen has is the right to be secure in his person, the right to be safe from physical or economic harm from another. Laws to protect citizens and advance the harmony of society are founded upon these principles. To enforce these laws, created in the best interest of society as a whole, there has to be a deterrent for a breach of the law. Therefore, deterrence is the first aim of a system of punishment.

Deterrence is only one side of the punishment coin, however. An equally fundamental reason to punish lies in society's compelling desire to see justice done. Punishment expresses the emotions of the society wronged, the anger and outrage felt, and it solidifies and reinforces the goals, values, and norms of acceptable behavior in the society....

The deterrent effect of the death penalty is the favorite criticism of the opponents of capital punishment. The social scientists' studies have been mixed at best and there is no authoritative consensus on whether or not the death penalty deters anyone from committing a crime. Threats of punishment cannot and are not meant to deter everybody all of the time. They are meant to deter most people most of the time. Therefore, the death penalty can only be a deterrent if it is meted out with a reasonable degree of consistency. The deterrence effect lies in the knowledge of the citizenry that it will more likely than not be carried out if the named crime is committed.

Even if one is not fully convinced of the deterrent effect of the death penalty, he or she would surely choose the certainty of the convicted criminal's death by execution over the possibility of the deaths of new victims.

Death penalty opponents argue that if life is sacred, then the murderer's life, too, is sacred ... and for the State to punish him by execution is barbaric and causes the State to bend to the murderer's level. The only similarity between the unjustified taking of an innocent life and the carrying out of a convicted murder's execution is the end result — death. The death penalty is a legal sentence, enacted by the legislatures of various states which presumably reflect their constituents' desires. It is a penalty that can finally be carried out only after a trial where the defendant is afforded all of his constitutional rights....

Death penalty opponents are also troubled by the studies that purport to show that the death penalty is applied capriciously, that it discriminates racially and economically.... Assuming that premise for the sake of argument, is that a rational reason to abolish the death penalty? Is the fact that some guilty persons escape punishment sufficient to let all guilty persons escape it?

... If the death penalty can deter one murder of an innocent life or if it can make a statement to the community about what will and will not be tolerated, then it is justified.

Opponents of the death penalty advocate the life sentence in prison as a viable alternative to execution.... Early release programs, furloughs, and escape combine to place a shockingly high number of convicted murderers back on the streets in record time.

The life without parole sentence is no solution either. First the possibility of escape cannot be completely eliminated, even in the most secure of institutions.... Second, the life without parole sentence places a tremendous burden on prison administrators. Faced with controlling inmates who have already received the worst punishment society can mete out, they can only throw their hands up in frustration. Lastly, the true lifer is not only capable of continuing to murder, but may actually be more likely to do so. Every prison in the country has its own stories of the lifer who killed another inmate over a cigarette or a piece of chicken.

STATEMENT OF ROBERT B. KLIESMET, PRESIDENT, INTERNATIONAL UNION OF POLICE ASSOCIATIONS, BEFORE THE SENATE JUDICIARY COMMITTEE, SEPTEMBER 19, 1989.

Street cops, in their pragmatic view, believe, as does 86 percent of the public, that the death penalty is a viable deterrent for persons convicted of certain crimes. A search of the literature shows there are a number of studies and articles that show a direct deterrent effect by imposing and carrying out the death penalty. One study goes as far as to point out that for each execution for a homicide, up to 15 lives can be saved through the deterrent effect. The safety of society, which is the real goal of the criminal justice system, is being compromised by saving the life of a convicted offender. This compromise is a needless sacrifice of a blameless victim's life.

PREPARED STATEMENT OF NEWT GINGRICH (R-GA), JANUARY 31, 1988.

... [The state] should use the death penalty for such serious crimes as murder and treason. Criminals might think twice before committing such acts if they knew that the consequences of their actions could result in the death penalty. People must be held accountable for the crimes they commit. I don't believe we can just slap someone on the hand and hope they never misbehave again.

Right now there are over a thousand prisoners on death row. Many of them have been there since the early 1970s because our current criminal justice system encourages them to seek endless appeals in order to delay their sentence of death.

I believe this is wrong. That's why I'm working on legislation to establish a unified appeals process that would place a two-year time limit on appeals to federal courts. This would prevent persons convicted of crimes from deliberately dragging out their appeals simply to delay the death sentence.

PREPARED STATEMENT OF SENATOR JOHN P. EAST (R-NC), JANUARY 16, 1986.

With the tougher attitude towards crime that we have taken in the past five years, the murder rate has gone down, but day after day we still read newspaper accounts of murders, many of which are carried out with chilling cruelty and detachment. The American people deserve continued protection from this wave of killing, protection often denied them by a system that often still gives lenient penalties to the most vicious criminals.

Death is the only suitable penalty for reprehensible crimes such as premeditated murder. Murder does not simply differ in magnitude from extortion or theft. It differs in kind as well, and its punishment also should differ in kind. Murderers have not simply injured their victims, but they have weakened the most important bond that holds communities together — respect for life. By imposing the supreme penalty in cases of murder, society expresses its moral outrage at such a crime; it sends a signal that innocent human life is precious; and it declares that such life cannot be violated without a like consequence to the killer. By imposing the death penalty, it also deters other would-be murderers, and it prevents the murderer from killing again.

I am convinced that there needs to be a Federal death penalty statute. In particular, we need to be able to impose the death penalty for the assassination of high government officials. We also need to provide for capital punishment in cases where convicted killers, already confined in a Federal prison and serving life sentences, commit murder again. At present, such people have no incentive not to kill because they are already suffering the severest penalty that Federal law has to offer. As a result, the number of gruesome murders at Federal correctional institutions is on the rise.

TESTIMONY OF ROSCOE STOVALL, PRESIDENT AND LEGISLATIVE COUNSEL, PROTECT THE INNOCENT, INDIANAPOLIS, INDIANA, BEFORE THE SENATE JUDICIARY COMMITTEE, APRIL 10, 1981.

An Englishman by the name of Sir James Stephen put it in proper perspective when he said, "The fact that men are hanged for murder is one reason why murder is considered to be so dreadful a crime." Life is cheapened if we don't place a higher penalty on the taking of a life than we do on mere property crimes.

Our organization represents victims of crime around the country as well as people, all of us, who are potential crime victims. Why such a concern by a few over the death penalty? The citizen deserves to live without the threat of violence. Capital punishment is the only perhaps final measure that society has of protection from those violent criminals who plague society. The life of man is and should be sacred, so sacred that each man's right to live should be secure.

Police Chief Ed Davis once said, "You don't shoot a rabid dog to deter other rabid dogs; you shoot him so he won't bite somebody." That is the very harsh reality that we have to contend with, that in fact isolation of that person from humanity may be important.

TESTIMONY OF WALTER BERNS, RESIDENT SCHOLAR, AMERICAN ENTERPRISE INSTITUTE FOR PUBLIC POLICY RESEARCH BEFORE THE SENATE JUDICIARY COMMITTEE, MAY 1, 1981.

My argument in favor of capital punishment is not primarily a deterrence argument. The evidence on this question — that is to say, whether executions have a differential deterrence capacity or whether they, better than imprisonment, serve to deter potential murderers, for example — that evidence is disputed. You will be told that executions do not deter; that social science evidence demonstrates that executions do not deter, or do not deter any better than imprisonment; or that there is no evidence that they do.

You will also be referred to the sophisticated studies of Isaac Erlich which conclude that an execution may deter as many as eight murders. I, quite frankly, do not know who is right — Erlich or his many critics. My opinion, however, is — but I stress that it is only an opinion — that in our present situation when, as I calculate it, and I did this in the book, 97.5 percent of the crimes committed in this country go unpunished, it would be foolish to expect to find that punishment of any sort deters. The fact is crime pays and criminals know it, and they act accordingly.

Crime, of course, does not pay for some. They end up in prison. But, one suspects that those who end up in prison are the not-so-intelligent or the unlucky.

Now I am not saying ... that there is no moral case to be made against capital punishment. There surely is. It has traditionally been imposed in this country in a grossly discriminatory fashion. It remains to be seen whether this country can impose the death penalty without regard to race or class. If we cannot, if we impose it on poor blacks and send our rich white murderers to prison, the death penalty will have to be invalidated on equal protection grounds.

My moral argument briefly goes as follows. I will list a number of points here and go over them as briefly as I can:

One, we punish in part for retributive reasons, which is to say we want to pay the criminal back.

Two, this desire to pay back arises out of our anger and the moral indignation that accompanies that anger.

Three, anger, while of course it has to be tamed, has to be calmed —and that is, of course, one function of the law—anger is altogether proper. A society without anger or without citizens capable of being angry when their fellow citizens are the victims of criminals, a society consisting entirely of Kitty Genovese's neighbors — and I assume the reference to Kitty Genovese is understood. She was the poor victim of a crime in Queens — I forget how many years ago, about 15 probably — who was mugged and eventually murdered. Many people heard her screaming in the night and no one came to her assistance and no one even bothered to call the police. As I say, a society consisting entirely of people like that, people like Kitty Genovese's neighbors, would be a society not worth living in. No one would care for anyone else. It would be a wholly selfish society.

Four, anger aroused by the sight of crime committed against others is a sign of caring for others. That anger is a sign of caring for others.

Five, in this respect it resembles love and is like love and is dissimilar to jealousy or greed, two human passions that are, I think, wholly selfish. Anger, like love, is not wholly selfish.

Six, the law should respect such anger. In fact, the law as one of its functions should satisfy that anger.

Seven, the law satisfies that anger when it punishes the object of that anger, the criminal.

Eight, when it satisfies that anger it rewards it, it justifies it. The law says, in effect, to be angry in such circumstances is to demonstrate a sense of and a desire for justice.

Nine, by rewarding the anger the law promotes law-abidingness; it promotes good habits. It has what a Norwegian criminologist, Johannes Andenaes, calls a "general deterrent effect"; that is, it deters crime not by instilling fear, the fear of punishment, although as I say it may do that, but it deters by rewarding such anger. It inculcates law-abiding habits.

Quoting from a book written by Berns, "Capital punishment, like banishment in other times and places, serves a similar purpose: It reminds us, or can remind us, of the reign of the moral order, and enhances, or can enhance, its dignity. The law must not be understood to be merely statutes that we enact or repeal at our pleasure and obey or disobey at our convenience, especially not the criminal law. Whenever law is regarded as merely statutory, by which I mean arbitrary or enacted out of no moral necessity or reflecting no law beyond itself," when that happens, "people will soon enough disobey it, and the clever ones will learn to do so with impunity." Somehow we in this country have to understand that crime is wrong and that the taking of a human life is a terrible, terrible crime. The law, I argue, must somehow inculcate that in our hearts and minds.

TESTIMONY OF ERNEST VAN DEN HAAG, ADJUNCT PROFESSOR OF SO-CIAL PHILOSOPHY, NEW YORK UNIVER-SITY , BEFORE THE SUBCOMMITTEE ON CRIMINAL LAW AND PROCEDURES OF THE SENATE JUDICIARY COMMITTEE, MARCH 15, 1972.

It is suggested that the death penalty discriminates against the poor and the black.... If true ... the suggestion would be nonetheless wholly irrelevant. It concerns the unfair way in which the penalty is distributed, not the fairness or unfairness of the penalty.

Any penalty ... could be unfairly or unjustly applied. The vice is not in the penalty, but in the process by which it is inflicted. It is unfair to inflict unequal penalties on equally guilty parties, or on any innocent parties, regardless of what the penalty is ... you should try to correct the judicial processes by which, it is alleged, the penalties are unfairly inflicted....

All penalties — including fines, prison sentences, and the death penalty — are deterrent roughly in proportion to their severity.... Were that not the case, we would certainly not have varied penalties, but might impose a uniform penalty of $5 for any crime whatsoever. We impose penalties roughly differentiated because we feel that crimes of different gravity deserve different punishment.

On the basis of the statistics available, no logical conclusion one way or the other can be reached. It cannot be proven that the death penalty is additionally deterrent; it cannot be proven either that it is not....

No penalty can deter the irrational, perhaps. But penalties do influence those who are rational enough to be influenced. In this respect the data suggest the death penalty has been very effective, precisely because very few murders are committed by rational persons.

CHAPTER XI

THE DEBATE — CAPITAL PUNISHMENT SHOULD BE ABOLISHED

STATEMENT OF REPRESENTATIVE HENRY B. GONZALEZ (D-TX) IN THE HOUSE OF REPRESENTATIVES, JUNE 30, 1995.

... I believe that the death penalty is an act of vengeance veiled as an instrument of justice. Not only do I believe that there are independently sufficient moral objections to the principle of capital punishment to warrant its abolition, but I also know that the death penalty is meted out to the poor, to a disproportionate number of minorities, and does not either deter crime or advance justice.

At a time when South Africa's highest court, in the first ruling of the new multiracial Constitutional Court, has just abolished the death penalty — on grounds that it is a cruel and inhumane punishment that does not deter crime but which does cheapen human life — as part of the post-apartheid quest for democratic government and a just society in that country, we should live up to no lower of a standard in our continuing effort to uphold democracy and justice in our own land.

Violent crimes have unfortunately become a constant in our society. Every day people are robbed, raped, and murdered. We are surrounded by crime and yet feel helpless in our attempt to deter, to control, and to punish. The sight of any brutal homicide excites a passion within us that demands retributive justice. We have difficulty comprehending that which cannot be understood..., we will never comprehend the rationale of violent crime, but the atrocity of the crime must not cloud our judgment and we must not let our anger undermine the wisdom of our rationality. We cannot allow ourselves to punish an irrational action with an equally irrational retaliation — murder is wrong, whether it is committed by an individual or by the State.

Violence begets violence.... Indeed, I wonder whether the overall escalation of violence in our society perpetrated by criminals can be traced to the devaluation of human life as exhibited by our governments.

The United Nations Universal Declaration of Human Rights states, "No one shall be subjected to torture or to cruel, inhuman or degrading treatment or punishment." The death penalty is torture, and numerous examples exist emphasizing the cruelty of the execution. Witness Jimmy Lee Gray, who was executed in 1983 in the Mississippi gas chamber. During his execution he struck his head repeatedly on the pole behind him and had convulsions for 8 minutes.... Witness the execution by lethal injection of James Autry in 1984.... He took ten minutes to die, and during much of that period he was conscious and complaining of pain.

... proponents insist that it fulfills some social need. This simply is not true. Studies fail to establish that the death penalty either has a unique value as a deterrent or is a more effective deterrent than life imprisonment. We assume that perpetrators will give greater consideration to the consequences of their actions if the penalty is death, but the problem is that we are not always dealing with rational actions. Those who commit violent crimes often do so in moments of passion, rage, and fear — times when irrationality reigns.

... If a murderer deserves death, I ask why then do we not burn the arsonist or rape the rapist? Our justice system does not provide for such punishments because society comprehends that it must be founded on principles different from those it condemns. How can we condemn killing while condoning execution?

In practice capital punishment has become a kind of grotesque lottery. It is more likely to be carried out in some States than in others.... The death penalty is far more likely to be imposed against blacks than whites.... It is most likely to be imposed upon the poor and uneducated — 60 percent of death row inmates never finished high school....

There are moves on in Congress to speed up the execution process by limiting and streamlining the appeals process. But when the statistics show how arbitrarily the death penalty is applied, how can we make any changes without first assuring fairness.... There are no do-overs in this business when mistakes are made....

EXCERPTS FROM JUSTICE HARRY A. BLACKMUN'S OPINION DISSENTING FROM THE SUPREME COURT'S ORDER DENYING REVIEW IN A TEXAS DEATH PENALTY CASE, FEBRUARY 23, 1994.

Twenty years have passed since this Court declared that the death penalty must be imposed fairly, and with reasonable consistency or not at all and despite the effort of the states and courts to devise legal formulas and procedural rules to meet this daunting challenge, the death penalty remains fraught with arbitrariness, discrimination, caprice and mistake....

Experience has taught us that the constitutional goal of eliminating arbitrariness and discrimination from the administration of death can never be achieved without compromising an equally essential component of fundamental fairness: individualized sentencing....

For more than 20 years I have endeavored — indeed, I have struggled, along with a majority of this Court — to develop procedural and substantive rules that would lend more than the mere appearance of fairness to the death penalty endeavor. Rather than continue to coddle the Court's delusions that the desired level of fairness has been achieved and the need for regulation eviscerated, I feel morally and intellectually obligated simply to concede that the death penalty experiment has failed. It is virtually self-evident to me now that no combination of procedural rules or substantive regulations ever can save the death penalty from its inherent constitutional deficiencies. The problem is that the inevitability of factual, legal, and moral error gives us a system that we know must wrongly kill some defendants, a system that fails to deliver the fair, consistent and reliable sentence of death required by the Constitution....

[There would be no] constitutional dilemma if fairness to the individual could be achieved without sacrificing the consistency and rationality promised in *Furman* [see Chapter II]. While one might hope that providing the sentencer with as much relevant mitigating evidence as possible will lead to more rational and consistent sentences, experience has taught otherwise. It seems that the decision whether a human being should live or die is so inherently subjective, rife with all of life's understandings, experiences, prejudices and passions, that it inevitably defies the rationality and consistency required by the Constitution.

OPENING STATEMENT OF SENATOR HOWARD M. METZENBAUM (D-OH) BEFORE THE SENATE JUDICIARY COMMITTEE, APRIL 1, 1993.

My principal reason for opposing the death penalty is my concern that an innocent person might be sentenced to death, as happened on too many occasions in the past. I am not here to say that scores of the 2,000 people who are on death row are innocent, but if there are only half a dozen, or even one, that is one too many. When the Government punishes an individual with death, there is no margin for error.

... Being concerned about executing an innocent person is not the same as being soft on crime. Instead it is a matter of ensuring the fairness, integrity and reliability of our criminal justice system at the moment at which it inflicts the ultimate penalty.

STATEMENT OF SENATOR CAROL MOSELEY-BRAUN (D-CA) BEFORE THE SENATE JUDICIARY COMMITTEE, APRIL 1, 1993.

... the Supreme Court's recent holding in the *Herrera* case [see Chapter III], that a death row inmate's claim of actual innocence does not entitle him to *habeas* relief, is deeply troubling in an era when Congress and State legislatures are rushing to make more and more crimes punishable by death yet simultaneously curtailing the right to appeal at both the State and Federal levels....

When human judgment becomes infallible, our system will be infallible. Until then, those who would strip the system of vital safeguards lead us ever closer to the day when we in the name of the State we will execute an innocent man. And that, in the word of justice [sic] Brennan's dissent in the *Herrera* case, "comes perilously close to simple murder."

STATEMENT OF WALTER MCMILLIAN, MONROEVILLE, ALABAMA, BEFORE THE SENATE JUDICIARY COMMITTEE, APRIL 1, 1993.

My name is Walter Mcmillian. I was sentenced to die in the electric chair and spent nearly six years on Death Row in Alabama awaiting execution for a murder that I did not commit, a murder that I knew nothing about, a murder that I had nothing to do with. Today, the State of Alabama has acknowledged that I am an innocent man and that I was wrongfully convicted. What happened to me could have happened to you, or to anyone else. I was convicted and sentenced to death on the false testimony of one man. I am here today to urge you to do all that is in your power to prevent what happened to me from happening to anyone else.

PREPARED STATEMENT OF GARY PARKER, GEORGIA STATE SENATOR, FIFTEENTH SENATORIAL DISTRICT, COLUMBUS, GA, HOUSE JUDICIARY COMMITTEE, MAY 9, 1990.

For the past two decades, I have witnessed our country resort to increasingly desperate measures to fight the war on crime. We are making greater use of incarceration [and] mandatory sentencing. We now have many more persons incarcerated than ever before ... our prison population in Georgia is expected to triple in the next ten years....

... Columbus is one of the jurisdictions which has most often imposed the death penalty in Georgia — 17 death sentences have been handed down in the judicial circuit that includes Columbus since the resumption of capital punishment in Georgia. This is five more death sentences than have been imposed during the same period in the circuit that includes Atlanta, which has over twice the population of our circuit.

Despite all these anti-crime measures, when I ask my constituents whether they feel safer today than they felt a decade age, nearly everyone responds with a resounding "no." I have little doubt but that our past efforts to deal with the crime issue — by building more prisons and by constricting our civil and constitutional rights — amount to a near complete failure.

... The death penalty has symbolic and political value to politicians, but it has no value to black neighborhoods that are plagued with violent crime. Concentration of resources on a few high profile capital cases helps a prosecutor, attorney general, or governor get reelected or advance to higher office, but it hurts the fight against crime by diverting resources from hundreds of other cases, as well as from problems that are affecting the day-to-day lives of the black community.

... Instead of attacking the problems which result in many young African-Americans becoming involved in crime, our criminal justice system waits until tragedy strikes and responds by sentencing a few young men to death to show how mad we are. We have expensive show trials and years of costly litigation over the appropriateness of the death penalty for a few offenders. This is not protecting our community from violent crime. One capital case now pending in Columbus involves a young black man who suffers from schizophrenia who walked into the police headquarters in broad daylight and, in the presence of a number of officers, opened fire, killing one officer.

... This young man has a long history of severe mental illness. Sentencing him to death will not prevent another mentally disturbed person from causing some other tragedy.

... the death penalty has not been justly imposed. One of the most obvious examples is the case of a mentally retarded black man who was executed after being sentenced to death by an all-white jury for the murder of a white person. Executing this man was like executing a ten-year-old child.

TESTIMONY OF JULIUS L. CHAMBERS, DIRECTOR-COUNSEL, NAACP LEGAL DEFENSE AND EDUCATIONAL FUND, INC., HOUSE JUDICIARY COMMITTEE, MARCH 14, 1990.

... passage of the proposed death penalty bills would not advance — but would instead retard — resolution of the vexing problems associated with urban crime. While holding up the mirage of fighting and deterring crime, these death penalty bills would surely result in furthering the historical and well-documented racial disparities in the imposition of capital punishment in the United States.

Our concern is squarely grounded in the stark reality which black people have traditionally faced. For more than three centuries, the weight of the death penalty in this country has been borne far more heavily by blacks than by whites....

Since executions resumed in 1977, racial bias has remained inseparable from imposition of the death penalty. In this period, 121 persons have been executed. Of them, 49 or 41 percent have been black; 100, or 83 percent, have been executed for the murder of a white victim. After evaluating 28 studies, the GAO [Government Accounting Office] concluded that in 82 percent of the studies, the race of the victim "was found to influence the likelihood of being charged with capital murder or receiving the death penalty; i.e., those who murdered whites were found to be more likely to be sentenced to death than those who murdered blacks." The GAO found this conclusion held true even after controlling statistically for other factors thought to influence the likelihood of receiving the death penalty.

... There is no question that the financial cost of sentencing a single person to death is astronomical.... For example, the GAO noted that one study done on "death penalty costs in New York estimated it would cost at least $1.8 million to defend and prosecute a capital case." By contrast, the cost of feeding and housing the defendant convicted in that same case for a period of 40 years would only be $602,000. The proposed statutes are absolutely silent as to where the millions of dollars would come from to "foot the bill." ...

Perhaps the true purpose of the bills is to divert the public's attention away from considering measures which could truly serve to fight crime. One commentator correctly observed that "... the death penalty debate enables public officials and legislators to falsely assert that they are being tough on crime because they favor the death penalty." More emphasis should be placed on the less glamorous side of fighting crime. Most major cities in the country, for example, cannot afford to offer adequate treatment to young offenders who have become ensnared with the drug world....

It is a sad irony that among the Western democracies, America stands virtually alone in permitting capital punishment. It has been abolished throughout Western Europe, and nearly half of all nations have abolished the death penalty in law or in practice. But while Romania has abolished this barbaric form of punishment and South Africa ... has put a halt on all executions, Congress, in the spirit of the social control we criticize in China and Iran, has been able to find no greater solution to the problems of crime in the United States than these proposed death penalty statutes.

TESTIMONY OF HENRY SCHWARZ-CHILD, DIRECTOR, AMERICAN CIVIL LIBERTIES UNION (ACLU) CAPITAL PUNISHMENT PROJECT, BEFORE THE HOUSE JUDICIARY COMMITTEE, MARCH 14, 1990.

The American Civil Liberties Union ... hold[s] capital punishment to be inherently cruel and unusual punishment, barred by the Eighth Amendment to the Constitution. We conclude, furthermore, that in its application the death penalty violates the due-process-of-law clause of the Fifth Amendment and the equal-protection-of-the-law clause of the Fourteenth. These judgments are grounded in the evidence that the retention of the death penalty in no way contributes to a lessening of the incidence of violent crime, that executions are a barbaric spectacle inflicted upon isolated individual criminal offenders in circumstances redolent with arbitrariness, racial and sex discrimination as well as status bigotry, that entirely innocent persons are unavoidably executed on occasion and that the death penalty is not only staggeringly expensive to administer but radically distorts the entire scheme of criminal sentencing.

At least equally compelling is the almost universally shared sense that governments that use premeditated, violent homicides as instruments of social policy are a good deal less than civilized and enlightened and can hardly boast of their leadership in the advancing cause of human rights in the world. It is quite telling that the first act of several governments now newly emerging from political and racial tyranny has been the abolition or suspension of capital punishment — witness the recent promulgations of abolition or suspension in Romania and in the Republic of South Africa.

No one — I want to emphasize — opposes the death penalty because we think that violent crime is not so terrible or that punishment for it should not be proportionately severe. It is the *limits* of severity that is in controversy, not deep anguish about violent crime; that latter, we all, of course, share. When 200 years ago Western countries, including ours, abolished medieval forms of criminal punishment — drawing and quartering, boiling in oil, burning at the stake, gibbeting, and their like — we did so not because crimes were no longer thought to be so bad or because criminals had become nicer people: Those brutal forms of execution were abolished because we had come to think of *ourselves* as too civilized to do that sort of thing to another human being, no matter who he or she was or what they had done. *That*, and not the baseless claim that execution makes for less crime, is the issue. And that is true all the more at the end of an extremely bloody century, in which governments have killed uncounted numbers of human beings and from which we should have learned that governmental institutions do not have the moral right, should not have the legal power, to decide who lives and who dies. Almost every country abroad with whom we share moral and social and legal values has abolished the death penalty.... In sum: The civilized world looks with amazement and alienation at the United States, which holds some 2,500 human beings in its custody and proposes to kill them and in which the United States Congress now proposes to broaden the reach of capital punishment under federal law, among other things, even to non-homicidal crimes.

STATEMENT OF ERIC N. FREEDMAN, PROFESSOR, HOFSTRA UNIVERSITY SCHOOL OF LAW, HEMPSTEAD, NY, BEFORE THE HOUSE JUDICIARY COMMITTEE, MAY 23, 1990.

... [capital punishment] is counterproductive because the death penalty is a racially discriminatory panacea that does not work. It doesn't deter. That is not because of recent delays in its implementation. That has been shown in studies going back to the founding of this country. That has been shown historically over many centuries.

... to centralize the enormous power of the death penalty here in Washington is a serious and dangerous step. In every country where that power resides at the national level it has been abused for political reasons, and it can happen here.

You know more than anyone how Washington is subject to gusts of political passion so strong that no politician can stand in their way. It is not at all hard to imagine such a gust leading to one or more wrongful executions. And it is not hard to imagine a countergust that would then sweep away the death penalty altogether.

But the whole idea of decentralized government in this country is that the Government should be slower and surer than that. The Constitution was written in the recognition that crime is a socially destructive force, but that governmental abuse of power is far more destructive.

STATEMENT OF SENATOR EDWARD M. KENNEDY (D-MA), BEFORE THE SENATE JUDICIARY COMMITTEE, SEPTEMBER 19, 1989.

Government should not have the awesome law enforcement power to put a human being to death. No matter how brutal the crime a person has committed, the infliction of death at the hands of government brutalizes our society.

In my view, the death penalty is wrong as a matter of constitutional principle because it violates the Eighth Amendment's prohibition against cruel and unusual punishment....

The death penalty is also wrong because of the likelihood that innocent people will be executed. No system of justice, however wise or resourceful its judges and juries may be, can eliminate this risk. That is a risk we must accept when the punishment is imprisonment, because a jailed defendant can always be set free when innocence is proved. But that is a burden we cannot tolerate when the punishment is death.

Perhaps our answer would be different, if there was convincing evidence that the death penalty deters crime....

Some of the most convincing evidence that the death penalty does not deter is found in the experience of other Western democracies. Not one of those countries has capital punishment for peacetime crimes, and yet every one of them has a murder rate less than half that of the United States.

The death penalty is also fundamentally flawed in practice. Our long experience with capital punishment demonstrates that it is applied in an arbitrary and discriminatory manner. The Constitution requires that courts and juries be given discretion, within limits, in deciding whether or not a death sentence is appropriate for a particular defendant. The inevitable result is that persons who commit similar crimes are treated differently. All too often, that discretion has been abused in a racially discriminatory fashion.

... Racial discrimination in the application of capital punishment is intolerable in a country dedicated to equal justice under law. It is a blight on our judicial system.

STATEMENT OF RONALD E. HAMPTON, NATIONAL BLACK POLICE ASSOCIATION, BEFORE THE SENATE JUDICIARY COMMITTEE, SEPTEMBER 19, 1989.

As an advocacy organization for black police officers in America, we speak up and out against those issues that impact negatively on the black and poor communities. The National Black Police Association believes that the death penalty is unAmerican, unjust, and unconstitutional.

The death penalty in the United States includes the execution of juveniles, the execution of the mentally retarded, the execution of innocent individuals and racial bias.... However, how can murder, whether committed by the government or by an individual, ever be justified?...

And after eighteen years as a law enforcement officer, I have yet to witness *any crime* that warrants the death penalty. Violence only begets violence.

Proponents of the death penalty suggest that capital punishment means fewer murders, especially of police officers. FBI statistics for the period 1976-1987 prove just the opposite. In the twelve states where executions take place, the murder rate is 105 people per million, exactly twice the murder rate of the thirteen states without the death penalty. More police officers are killed in states with the death penalty than in states without it.

There is no scientific proof to support execution's effectiveness versus long-term imprisonment. The state of Michigan has not had a death penalty since 1846. Its homicide rate is no higher than that of Ohio which has a death penalty.

Texas, California, and Florida lead the nation in numbers of capital punishment cases. Yet all these states have experienced significant increases in homicides from 1965 to the present.

The death penalty is not justice, not a deterrent, not retribution — it is vengeance. Once a life has been taken, there is no restitution.

The death penalty makes irrevocable any possible miscarriage of justice. It has been documented that at least 25 Americans who were later found innocent have been executed in this country. The death penalty has killed an innocent person in the U.S. once every year since 1910. If just one innocent person dies, who among us can claim justice has been served?

The National Black Police Association believes that executions set a dehumanizing example of brutality that only encourages violence....

REVEREND GUILLERMO CHAVEZ, CHAIRMAN, NATIONAL INTERRELIGIOUS TASK FORCE ON CRIMINAL JUSTICE, BEFORE THE HOUSE JUDICIARY COMMITTEE, NOVEMBER 7, 1985.

... I question the notion of "standards of decency" as an accepted rationale upon which to base public policy. We need to remember that about 200 years ago, slaveholding was not considered offensive to the then current "standards of decency."

... As people of religious and ethical conscience, we seek the restoration and the renewal of wrongdoers, not their deaths. Capital punishment makes it possible for human error or prejudice to send innocent persons to their death. It eliminates forever the healing possibilities of human love and respect. Penal history provides us with prominent examples of innocent persons falsely condemned. Our Judeo-Christian heritage affirms that for the state to assume the power of absolute judgment is to assume a power that belongs only to God.

Another issue that concerns us is that the value of life, when confronted with the death penalty, is cheapened. In this regard, we are especially concerned with what the death penalty does to a society that inflicts it.

As the United Presbyterian Church has declared, "the use of the death penalty tends to brutalize the society that condones it." In denying the humanity of those we put to death, even those guilty of the most terrible crimes, including espionage or treason, we deny our own humanity and life is further cheapened. Nothing is achieved by taking one more life or adding one more victim.

RABBI IRWIN M. BLANK, ISAAC C. ROSENTHAL PROFESSOR OF JEWISH EDUCATION, BALTIMORE HEBREW COLLEGE, ON BEHALF OF THE SYNAGOGUE COUNCIL OF AMERICA, BEFORE THE HOUSE JUDICIARY COMMITTEE, NOVEMBER 7, 1985.

Our opposition to the death penalty is based both on our judgment as to the demands of contemporary American democratic standards and our Jewish tradition. This statement may seem surprising in view of the many references in our Bible to the death penalty for such transgressions as adultery, bestiality, murder, and the rape of a betrothed woman. Indeed, these Scriptural provisions are often invoked by defenders of capital punishment.

However, such defenses reflect an unfamiliarity with the full Jewish tradition, and specifically with the fact that rabbinic Judaism during the Talmudic period, some 2,000 years ago, represents the interpretation and implementation of the Scriptural command. We can fully understand the Scriptures only through their presentation of the oral law, of which the Talmud is the prime exponent. The definition and the application of the laws of evidence and criminal procedure in the Talmud made conviction in a capital case practically impossible. Thus, for example, it is noted that if an accused were to be convicted in a capital case the verdict had to be unanimous, the reasoning of the rabbis being that if not a single one of the 23 judges constituting the court, the Sanhedrin, could find some reason for acquittal, there was something fundamentally wrong with the court. Circumstantial evidence was not sufficient to sustain a verdict in a capital case; two eyewitnesses, subjected to rigorous cross-examination by the court, were required. Moreover, to assure that the act had been committed with full premeditation, both witnesses had to testify that they warned the accused before the crime that the act was prohibited and what its penal consequences were.

In view of these procedural requirements it is evident that conviction in a capital case was virtually impossible. But perhaps most indicative of the rabbinic view of capital punishment is the following from the Talmud, and I quote these citations:

> A Sanhedrin which executes a criminal once in seven years is called a "court of destroyers." Rabbi Eliezer ben Azariah states that this is so even if it executes one every 70 years. Rabbi Tarphon and Rabbi Akiba stated that if they had been members of the Sanhedrin, no one would have ever been executed.

... To take a human life, the rabbis said, is a matter of the gravest seriousness. Execution is not reversible. If a mistake is made, what has been done cannot be undone. One who takes a human life, they pointed out, diminishes the Divine image. On occasions, this extreme means may be necessary to protect society. But it may be carried out only when there can be absolutely no doubt concerning the guilt of the accused and of his freely chosen, deliberate, and knowing act. And historically, we find that all of the discussions say that that is virtually impossible to achieve. . . .

A note on a statement by an earlier witness on the attempt to eliminate capriciousness and fallibility — I would say that the whole rabbinic method of applying rigorous reasoning in all areas involving law is indicative of the fact that the rabbinic mind — and I think Judaism generally — does not place great store in our capacity to eliminate capriciousness and fallibility,....

REMARKS OF SUPREME COURT JUSTICE THURGOOD MARSHALL AT A JUDICIAL CONFERENCE OF THE SECOND CIRCUIT IN HERSHEY, PA, SEPTEMBER 6, 1985.

... capital defendants frequently suffer the consequences of having trial counsel who are ill-equipped to handle capital cases. Death penalty litigation has become a specialized field of practice, and even the most well-intentioned attorneys often are unable to recognize, preserve, and defend their client's rights. Often trial counsel simply are unfamiliar with the special rules that apply in capital cases. Counsel — whether appointed or retained — often are handling their first criminal cases, or their first murder cases, when confronted with the prospect of a death penalty. Though acting in good faith, they inevitably make very serious mistakes.... The federal reports are filled with stories of counsel who presented *no* evidence in mitigation of their client's sentences because they did not know what to offer or how to offer it, or had not read the state's sentencing statute.

... The Court has not yet recognized that the right of effective assistance must encompass a right to counsel familiar with death penalty jurisprudence at the trial stage. Instead, in all but the most egregious [outstanding for undesirable qualities] case, a court cannot or will not make a finding of ineffective assistance of counsel because counsel has met what the Supreme Court has defined as a minimal standard of competence for criminal lawyers. As a consequence, many capital defendants find that errors by their lawyers preclude presentation of substantial constitutional claims, but that such errors — with the resulting forfeitures of rights — are not sufficient in themselves to constitute ineffective assistance.

Contrary to popular perceptions, all capital defendants have *not* spent years filing frivolous claims in federal courts. Many of these defendants have not yet filed *any* federal claims when their execution dates are set. We simply cannot allow this inaccurate view to blind us to reality, or to accept the hasty review process on the ground that defendants already have had the benefits of an untruncated review process. Until an execution date is set, and the situation becomes urgent, capital defendants simply have been unable to secure counsel.

Once the execution date is set, the race is on. Prisoners who have not yet sought state or federal *habeas corpus* relief have roughly one month to do so.... But the new attorney often has no knowledge of the record, has not met the client, and has only a few days to read hundreds of pages of transcripts and prepare a petition. This petition, hastily prepared, must include all claims that the defendant might raise, because subsequent petitions will likely be declared abusive of the process if they entertain collateral attacks....

IMPORTANT NAMES AND ADDRESSES

American Bar Association
(ABA)
Criminal Justice
1800 M St. NW
Washington, DC 20036
(202) 331-2260
FAX (202) 331-2220

American Civil Liberties Union
(ACLU)
122 Maryland Ave. NE
Washington, DC 20002
(202) 544-1681
FAX (202) 546-0738

Amnesty International U.S.A.
304 Pennsylvania Ave. SE
Washington, DC 20003
(202) 544-0200
FAX (202) 546-7142
New York Office:
322 Eighth Ave.
New York City, NY 10001
(212) 807-8400

Bureau of Justice Statistics
633 Indiana Ave. NW, #1142
Washington, DC 20531
(202) 307-0765
FAX (202) 307-5846

Bureau of Prisons
320 1st St. NW
Washington, DC 20534
(202) 307-3198
FAX (202) 514-6878

Commission on Civil Rights
624 9th St. NW, #700
Washington, DC 20425
(202) 376-7700
Complaints: (800) 552-6843
FAX (202) 376-7672

Department of Justice
Main Justice Building
10th St. and Constitution Ave. NW
Washington, DC 20530

(202) 514-2000
FAX (202) 514-4371

Federal Bureau of Investigation
10th St. and Pennsylvania Ave.
NW
Washington, DC 20535
(202) 324-3691

House Judiciary Committee
2141 Rayburn House Office
Bldg.
Washington, DC 20515
(202) 225-3951
FAX (202) 225-7682

International Association of
Chiefs of Police
515 N. Washington St.
Alexandria, VA 22314-2357
(202) 836-6767

Justice Research and Statistics
Association
444 N. Capital St. NW, #445
Washington, DC 20001-1512
(202) 624-8560
FAX (202) 624-5269

NAACP Legal Defense and
Educational Fund
99 Hudson St., Suite 1600
New York, NY 10013-2897
(212) 219-1900
FAX (212) 226-7592

National Association of Criminal Defense Lawyers
1627 K St. NW, 12th Floor
Washington, DC 20006
(202) 872-8688
FAX (202) 331-8269

National Criminal Justice
Reference Service
P.O. Box 6000
Rockville, MD 20857

(800) 732-3277
In Maryland (301) 251-5500

National District Attorney's
Association
99 Canal Center Plaza, #510
Alexandria, VA 22314
(703) 549-9222
FAX (703) 836-3195

National Institute of Justice
633 Indiana Ave. NW
Washington, DC 20531
(202) 307-2942
FAX (202) 307-6394

Rand Corporation
2100 M St. NW
Washington, DC 20037
(202) 296-5000
FAX 296-7960

Senate Judiciary Committee
Dirksen Senate Office Bldg.
Room 224
Washington, DC 20510
(202) 224-5225
FAX (202) 224-9102

The Sentencing Project
918 F St. NW, #501
Washington, DC 20004
(202) 628-0871
FAX (202) 628-1091

Supreme Court of the United
States
1 1st St. NE
Washington, DC 20543
(202) 479-3211

U.S. Sentencing Commission
1 Columbus Circle NE
#2-500 South Lobby
Washington, DC 20002-8002
(202) 273-4500
FAX (202) 273-4529

RESOURCES

The Department of Justice collects statistics on death-row inmates as part of its "National Prisoner Statistics" (NPS) program. Based on voluntary reporting, the NPS program collects and interprets data on state and federal prisoners. Begun by the Bureau of the Census in 1926, the program was transferred to the Bureau of Prisons in 1950, to the now-defunct Law Enforcement Assistance Administration (LEAA), and then to the Bureau of Justice Statistics (BJS) in 1979.

Since 1972, the Bureau of the Census, as the collecting agent for the LEAA and BJS, has had responsibility for compiling the relevant data. The Bureau of Justice Statistics annually prepares a bulletin titled *Capital Punishment* which provides an overview of capital punishment in the United States. It also periodically publishes selected findings, such as *Prison Sentences and Time Served for Violence* (Washington, DC, 1995). The Bureau of Justice Statistics *Sourcebook of Criminal Justice Statistics*, prepared by The Hindelang Criminal Justice Research Center of the State University at Albany, NY, is the most complete compilation of criminal justice statistics.

The NAACP Legal Defense and Educational Fund, Inc. (LDF) is a private institution maintaining statistics on capital punishment. The LDF is strongly opposed to the death penalty. Despite its title, LDF is not part of the National Association for the Advancement of Colored People, although it was founded by that organization. For over 30 years, the New York-based LDF has had a separate Board of Directors, program, staff, office, and budget. LDF statistics tend to run somewhat higher than those of the Bureau of Justice Statistics (BJS) because they count all those under sentence of death while the BJS counts only those who have arrived in prison. The LDF publishes "Death Row, U.S.A.," a periodic compilation of capital punishment statistics and information, including the names of all those currently on death row.

Amnesty International is the Nobel Prize-winning, human rights organization headquartered in London, England, that strongly opposes the death penalty. Amnesty International maintains information on the death penalty and torture throughout the world and periodically publishes its findings. Information Plus would like to thank Amnesty International for permission to use its data on capital punishment around the world.

Information Plus also thanks the National Opinion Research Center and the Gallup Organization for the use of their polls.